Teacher's Pack **2**

CONTEMPORARY TOPICS

Academic Listening and Note-Taking Skills

THIRD EDITION

Ellen Kisslinger

Michael Rost
SERIES EDITOR

D1315672

PEARSON
Longman

Contemporary Topics 2: High Intermediate
Academic Listening and Note-Taking Skills
Third Edition

Pearson Education, 10 Bank Street, White Plains, NY 10606

Staff credits: The people who made up the *Contemporary Topics 2* team, representing editorial, production, design, and manufacturing, are Rhea Banker, Danielle Belfiore, Dave Dickey, Christine Edmonds, Nancy Flaggman, Dana Klinek, Amy McCormick, Linda Moser, Carlos Rountree, Jennifer Stem, Leigh Stolle, Paula Van Ells, Kenneth Volcjak, and Pat Wosczyk.
Cover design: Ann France
Text composition: ElectraGraphics, Inc.
Text font: 11/13 Times

ISBN-10: 0-13-600515-2
ISBN-13: 978-0-13-600515-5

PEARSON LONGMAN ON THE WEB

Pearsonlongman.com offers online resources for teachers and students. Access our Companion Websites, our online catalog, and our local offices around the world.

Visit us at **www.pearsonlongman.com**.

Printed in the United States of America
3 4 5 6 7 8 9 10—OPM—14 13 12 11 10 09

CONTENTS

INTRODUCTION

The *Contemporary Topics* series provides a stimulating, content-based approach that helps students develop their listening, note-taking, and discussion skills while studying relevant topics. Each unit centers around a short academic lecture, with topics drawn from a range of disciplines.

The lectures feature engaging instructors with live student audiences, and take place in authentic lecture hall settings. The multimodal design of each lecture allows for various learning formats for DVD users, including audio- or video-only presentations, optional subtitling, Presentation Points slide support, and pop-up Coaching Tips.

In order to maximize the benefits of content-based instruction, the *Contemporary Topics* series has developed a carefully sequenced eight-step learning methodology. This introduction provides an overview of each of these steps.

Step 1: Connect to the Topic   *Estimated Time: 10 minutes* This opening section
invites students to activate what they already know about the unit topic by connecting it to their own experiences and beliefs. Typically, students fill out a short survey and compare answers with a partner. The teacher acts as a facilitator, having students share ideas about the topic before they explore it further.

Basic Procedure:

- Set the tone for the unit by talking about the image(s) on the page or related current news events.

- Read the introductory paragraph aloud, paraphrasing as necessary.

- Have students complete the survey/activity.

- Ask students to compare answers with a partner, or discuss answers casually as a class.

Methodology Focus: The actual content of students' responses in this initial activity is not as important as their attempt to understand and interact. It is important that all students participate in activating their ideas about the theme of the unit. This engagement helps set the tone of "active listening" throughout the unit. Having students compare answers with a partner helps ensure that every student is on task and thinking about the unit topic.

 ## Step 2: Build Your Vocabulary   *Estimated Time: 15 minutes* This section
familiarizes students with the key content words and phrases from the lecture. Each lecture contains 10–15 key words from the Academic Word List to ensure that students learn core vocabulary needed for academic success. Students read and *listen to* target words in context so that they can better prepare for the upcoming lecture. Students then complete exercises to get an initial understanding of the target lexis of the unit. Interact with Vocabulary! is a supplementary activity that focuses on the syntax and collocations of new vocabulary in the unit.

Basic Procedure:

- Have students listen to the sentences or paragraphs.

- Have students guess the meaning of each boldfaced word and choose the best definition.

- If time permits, try the Interact with Vocabulary! activity to enable students to focus on form as they learn new words and collocations.

Methodology Focus: Vocabulary knowledge and the ability to recognize vocabulary as it is spoken are key predictors of listening comprehension. As such, spending some pre-listening time on recognizing key vocabulary from the lecture will usually increase students' comprehension of the ideas in the lecture. It's best to spend 10–15 minutes on vocabulary preparation. More than this may give students the impression that vocabulary learning is overly important. Research shows that multiple exposures to new words in context is necessary for vocabulary acquisition, so it's not essential that students "master" the vocabulary in this section. Frequent reviews of the vocabulary sections will aid in acquisition.

 Step 3: Focus Your Attention *Estimated Time: 10 minutes* In this section, students learn strategies for listening actively and taking clear notes. Because a major part of "active listening" involves a readiness to deal with comprehension difficulties, this section provides specific tips to help students direct their attention and gain more control of how they listen. The Try It Out! section, based on a short audio extract, allows students to work on listening and note-taking strategies before they get to the main lecture. Typically, examples of actual notes are provided to give students concrete "starter models."

Basic Procedure:

- Go through this section carefully, reading explanations aloud. Draw attention to examples.

- Play the audio for Try It Out! in order to have students experience the given technique.

- After you play the audio extract once or twice, have students compare answers and/or notes with a partner.

Methodology Focus: Active listening involves a number of component strategies for focusing students' attention: predicting, guessing (i.e. using available knowledge to make good guesses), filling in gaps and making connections, monitoring areas where they don't understand, asking questions, and responding personally. Above all, active listening involves curiosity and a desire to understand more deeply. This section provides tips for focusing students' attention that, when learned incrementally, will help them become more active listeners. It is important that students find a specific way to control their attention and concentration as they listen.

 Step 4: Listen to the Lecture *Estimated Time: 20–30 minutes* As the central section of each unit, Listen to the Lecture allows for two full listening cycles: one to focus on "top-down listening" strategies (Listen for Main Ideas) and one to focus on "bottom-up listening" strategies (Listen for Details). In keeping with the principles of content-based instruction, students are provided with several layers of support. In the Before You Listen section, students are guided to activate concepts and vocabulary they already know or studied earlier in the unit.

The lecture can be viewed in video mode or just listened to in audio mode. In video mode, the lecture can be accompanied by the speaker's Presentation Points or by subtitles for reinforcing comprehension (recommended as a final review). Coaching Tips on strategies for listening, note-taking, and critical thinking can also be turned on.

Basic Procedure:

Before You Listen

- Have students go through this section explicitly—for instance, actually writing down a "prediction" when asked.

Listen for Main Ideas

- Have students *close their books* and take notes as they listen.
- Play the lecture through or pause at times. If pausing, it's best to do so at episode boundaries (see Audioscripts in this Teacher's Pack), as these are natural pausing points.
- Have students complete the exercise, working alone, using their notes.
- Check answers, or play the lecture again so students can confirm their answers. If repeating the lecture, have students confirm and expand their notes with books closed.

Listen for Details

- Play the lecture one more time, again with students confirming and expanding their notes. Then have students complete the Listen for Details exercise.

Methodology Focus: The lecture itself is the focal point of each unit, and therefore the focal point of the content-based approach. In this approach, students of course learn grammar, vocabulary, and pronunciation, but always within the context of relevant content, which may make it more memorable. We recommend that you focus on helping students understand the content of each lecture as deeply as possible, and work on specific language skills during the Talk about the Topic, Review Your Notes, and Extend the Topic sections. To better understand the lecture, students can work on two kinds of exercises: "Top-down listening" generally refers to "getting the gist" of what is said, not focusing on all of the details. "Bottom-up listening" generally refers to hearing "the signal"—that is, the exact words, intonations, and syntax that a speaker uses. Effective listening involves both kinds of processing. As teachers, we may naturally assume that "top-down" processing is more important, but research shows that skills in bottom-up processing is *a key determiner of progress* in L2 listening.

 Step 5: Talk about the Topic *Estimated Time: 15 min* Here students gain valuable discussion skills as they talk about the lecture. Discussion skills are an important part of academic success, and most students benefit from structured practice. In these activities, students listen to a short "model discussion" involving both native and non-native speakers, and identify the speaking strategies and gambits that are used. They then attempt to use some of those strategies in their own discussion groups.

Basic Procedure:

- Have students close their books and listen to the discussion.
- With books open, students may listen again and complete Parts A and B to show a basic understanding of the discussion. Alternatively, you can have students answer general comprehension questions: What was this discussion about? What happened in this discussion? etc.

- Next, have students work in groups of three to five, ideally. They should choose a topic and discuss. They should try to use the discussion strategies they have learned in this or previous units.

Methodology Focus: The first two activities in this section are awareness-raising: We want students to understand the content of the discussion *and* try to identify the types of "discourse strategies" that the study group students are using to make the discussion go well. Discussion ability involves a combination of verbal and nonverbal skills. If showing the video, encourage students to focus on the nonverbal actions of the student speakers: their body language (posture), gaze (direction of eyes on other speakers), and back-channeling (signals to show they are paying attention). Speaking strategies develop incrementally. It's important to have students try out different types of strategies in order to see how they may or may not help students express themselves more fully.

Step 6: Review Your Notes *Estimated Time: 15 minutes* Using notes for review and discussion is an important study skill that is developed in this section. Students are guided in reviewing the content of the unit, clarifying concepts, and preparing for the Unit Test. Incomplete, abbreviated examples of actual notes are provided to help students not only review for the test but also compare and improve their own note-taking skills.

Basic Procedure:

- Have students take out their notes and, with a partner, *take turns* explaining the ideas from the lecture.

- Then have them complete the partial notes.

- Ask if there are any questions about the lecture or anything in their notes. You may wish to preview the Unit Test to be sure that students have discussed the items that will be on it.

Methodology Focus: This section "completes the loop" on note-taking. Research shows that the value of note-taking for memory building is realized primarily when note-takers review their notes and attempt to reconstruct the content. By making explicit statements about the content of the lecture, students are "pushing" their output. They need to use precise grammar and vocabulary in order to articulate their ideas.

 ## Step 7: Take the Unit Test *Estimated Time: 15 minutes* This activity completes the study cycle of the unit: preparation, listening to the lecture, review of content, and assessment. The Unit Test, contained only in this Teacher's Pack, is to be photocopied and distributed by the teacher. Students complete it in class as they listen to the test questions on the audio CD. The *Contemporary Topics* tests are challenging—intended to motivate students to learn the material thoroughly. The format features an answer sheet with choices; the question "stem" is provided on audio only. Test-taking skills include verbatim recall, paraphrasing, inferencing, and synthesizing information from parts of the lecture.

Basic Procedure:

- Optional: Play the lecture once again.

- Pass out a copy of the Unit Test to each student and go over the directions.

- Play the audio for the test one time as students complete the test by circling their answers. You may pause the audio between questions.

- Collect the tests to correct yourself, or have students exchange papers and go over the answers in class. Replay the audio as you go over the correct answers.

Methodology Focus: The tests in *Contemporary Topics* have the question "stem" on audio only—the students can't read it. They have to listen carefully and then choose the correct answer. This format is more challenging than most standardized tests, such as the TOEFL. We chose this challenging format to motivate students to work through the unit diligently and know the content well.

 Step 8: Extend the Topic *Estimated time: 20 minutes* This final section creates a natural extension of the unit topic to areas that are relevant to students. Students first listen to a supplementary media clip drawn from a variety of interesting genres. Typically, students then have a discussion or prepare a class presentation.

Basic Procedure:

- Choose one of the activities, or more if time permits. Review the steps of the activity together.

- Allow time, if possible, for student presentations.

Methodology Focus: An important aspect of a content-based approach is the application, or follow-up step. This step helps students personalize the content of the unit, choosing to develop topics of personal interest. Allowing time for student research and presentations not only increases interest and involvement in the course, but also allows the teacher an opportunity to give individualized feedback that will help students' progress.

By completing these eight steps, students can develop stronger listening, speaking, and note-taking skills and strategies—thereby becoming more confident and independent learners.

Michael Rost
Series Editor

Multimedia Guidelines: With the DVD, you can play the lecture in different modes: video, video with subtitles, video with Coaching Tips, video with Presentation Points, video with Coaching Tips and subtitles, and video with Coaching Tips and Presentation Points. We do not recommend playing the video with both the Presentation Points and subtitles on.

Note that while the DVD is compatible with most computer media players, for optimum viewing we suggest playing the DVD on a television screen (ideally a wide-screen), using a DVD player.

You can also play the lecture as audio only, using the CD.

We recommend that you play the lecture once in "plain" video mode, then once as audio only. For review, you can play the video again with the Presentation Points and/or Coaching Tips turned on. As another review option, students can watch the subtitled version on their own.

Viewing preferences can be selected under SET UP. Or, with a remote control, subtitles can be activated at any time using the caption button, and Presentation Points can be activated at any time using the angle button.

TEACHING TIPS

UNIT OVERVIEW

In this unit, students will consider names as a cultural universal and the impact of a person's name in social situations. The lecture focuses on the four main ways parents determine names for their children. It also explores issues such as name stereotypes and selecting a name to avoid gender discrimination. Follow-up projects extend the topic to trends in names and name changes.

Connect to the Topic *page 2*   *~10 minutes*

As a warm-up activity, have students cover the photo captions and name the stars. Then ask students to guess the stars' real names. Students take a survey about names. Survey questions ask students to agree or disagree with statements about the importance of names. Students then compare responses and give reasons.

Build Your Vocabulary *pages 3–4*   *~15 minutes*

Students study these words and phrases related to sociology and names:

admire	example of	passed down
assignments	gender (neutral)	prime (example)
associated with	generations	qualifies as
benefit to	image	rely on
classic (name)	judged by	respond to
custom	named after	symbol (of identity)
discrimination	out of style	

For the Interact with Vocabulary! activity, encourage students to notice the boldfaced word in each sentence. When paired with the correct particle from the box, these words form collocations, which are valuable in building students' vocabulary and fluency.

Focus Your Attention *page 5*   *~10 minutes*

Students learn two basic reasons for taking lecture notes—to focus on main ideas and to review information later. They also learn some signal phrases lecturers use to focus on main ideas, and how to organize their notes based on these phrases:

*In the first half, **you'll hear about** . . .*
*In the second half, **we'll discuss** . . .*
*Today's lecture **will focus on** . . .*

*This afternoon **we'll look at** . . .*
***I'd like to begin with** the first category . . .*
*Today's lecture will be **divided into two parts** . .*

Listen to the Lecture *pages 6–7*   *~30 minutes*

Prior to listening to the unit lecture, students write their own ideas on two common ways parents choose names (Before You Listen). Students then listen to the lecture and answer multiple-choice questions (Listen for Main Ideas) and true/false questions (Listen for Details).
Lecture video time: 7 min. 9 sec.   Number of episodes: 7

BONUS ACTIVITY

After students have completed the Before You Listen activity, divide them into small groups. Ask them to explain where their names come from. If they don't know, have them guess. As a class, take a tally of the most common—and most unusual—ways students got their names.

Talk about the Topic *page 8*   *~20 minutes*

Four students—Mia, Manny, Hannah, and River—discuss the lecture. Part A focuses on matching these students with comments from the discussion. In Part B, your students work on these discussion strategies:

- Asking for opinions or ideas: ". . . It's a big responsibility for parents to choose . . . Don't you think?"
- Asking for clarification or confirmation: "You mean, it's the parents' responsibility to give good names?"

For Part C, students are encouraged to use the discussion strategies they've learned. They may use phrases from the student discussion and/or the Discussion Strategy box, or they may come up with their own. An option is to assign each topic to a different group and have each group share its findings with the class.
Student discussion video time: 1 min. 31 sec.

Review Your Notes *page 9*   *~15 minutes*

Using their notes, students work in pairs to focus on the main ideas of the lecture.

Take the Unit Test *Teacher's Pack page 7*   *~15 minutes*

You may want to play the lecture again just before giving the test. Students answer standard test questions about the content of the lecture. Specifically, the test covers the following: four ways parents choose names, some research about names, and stereotypes associated with some names.

Extend the Topic *pages 10–11*   *~30 minutes*

- Listening and Discussion: Students listen to and discuss an interview about trends in names.
- Reading and Discussion: Students read and discuss comments from parents about how they chose names.
- Research and Presentation: Students conduct additional research on name changes or related areas of interest, then present in small groups.

Focus Your Attention:
Try It Out! *page 5*

Speaker: Sociology is the science of studying society. In sociology, we study the behavior of people in social groups. Today's lecture will be divided into two parts. In the first half, I'll give you an overview of the various kinds of sociological research being done. For example, some sociologists study the effects of gender on a person's daily life. They ask, do men and women—boys and girls—have different experiences just because of their gender? Then, in the second half of the lecture, we'll focus in on a particular area of research: gender in the workplace. And we'll try to answer these questions: Does gender matter at work? Where do we find gender discrimination for women? What about for men? . . .

Listen for Main Ideas and Listen
for Details *pages 6–7*

Sociology lecturer: **E1** Good afternoon. The focus of today's Introduction to Sociology class is names. In sociology, we study social groups and how people interact and respond to each other. How we respond to names is an interesting study. For example, depending on if I say my name is *Alex*, or *Alexandra*, or *Dr. Shaw*, you might respond differently to me. Names are a prime example of what we call a "cultural universal." That means we all have names. And we all call each other by names. So, it's a practice we all share. Today's lecture will be divided into two halves. In the first half, you'll hear about four ways parents choose names. In the second half, we'll discuss whether or not our names influence how people respond to us in our daily lives. Before we go on, though, I want to quickly mention that the scope of my lecture is limited to names from the English language. However, we would take a similar approach to analyzing how parents choose names in any other language. **E2** So, without a doubt, our names are important symbols of identity. And for some people, important enough to change! So, let's look at the four typical ways parents choose first names. They're also called given names because the name is given to the child. OK, the first is to rely on custom. Parents may choose a name in order to pass it down from one generation to the next. For example, a baby girl is born, and the parents decide to call her *Sarah* because her grandmother's name is *Sarah*. Or, if it's a boy, in some families the first son is named after the father. So if the father's name is, say, *Thomas Proctor*, then the son will be *Thomas Proctor Junior* or *Thomas Proctor the Second*. I read a funny variation on this. In 2004, a new father, Jon Blake, didn't want to use "junior" or "the second." He was a software engineer, so, so he named his son *Jon Blake Version 2.0*. Talk about a true computer geek! **E3** The second way parents choose names is to name a child after someone the parents admire, such as a favorite teacher, a family friend, or even a famous athlete or movie star. The third way is to choose a name the parents feel will provide some social benefit to their child. For example, if they're concerned about gender discrimination, they may choose a name that works for either a boy or a girl. A name like *Taylor*, for example. Or my name, *Alex*. In fact, my parents told me they thought *Alex* might give me an advantage when I applied for jobs. Or, if a parent wants people to notice their child, they may choose an unusual name, like *Denali* or *Sky*. **E4** The fourth and most common way parents choose a name is simple: It's because they like it. They like the sound or the feeling it has, or it's a classic name. Now, what qualifies as "classic"? Well, classic means the name never goes out of style. It's a name that was popular in 1900, 1980, and it's still popular today. Examples of classic boys names are *Robert* and *Michael*. For girls, *Emily* and *Anna* are a couple of classic examples. To summarize: Parents choose names either based on custom, or after someone they admire, or to help their child socially. Or, the most common way, because they like it. **E5** Now I want to consider these questions: Does someone's name influence how other people respond to them? Does a person's name affect their chances for success in life? A lot of research has been done around these queries. Specifically, researchers have explored whether it's better to have a classic name, such as *Robert*, or an unusual name, like *Darvlin*. At this point, sociologists like myself don't agree which is better. We can't say for sure. We do know, though, that there are stereotypes associated with names. By this I mean, we hear a name, and an image comes to mind. Fair or not, this is what happens. People get judged by the name they have. Does anyone doubt that? **E6** Well, here's a convincing example: Researchers took a homework assignment and made photocopies. On half of the copies, they wrote the name *Michael*. On the other half, they wrote the name *Hubert*. (*Hubert*, by the way, is not a common name in English.) Then they asked teachers to grade the homework. Guess what happened? The teachers gave *Michael* high grades, and *Hubert* much lower grades. Why? It was the same homework, wasn't it? The researchers concluded that the name *Michael* had to be the only factor. It appeared that teachers held a stereotype that a boy named *Michael* was smarter than a boy named *Hubert*. As a result, they gave *Michael* higher grades. **E7** Let's recap now. In today's class, we looked at four ways parents choose first names: because of customs, after someone they admire, to help their child socially. And the most common—because they like the name. We also looked at research to answer the question: Does a name matter? In your study groups, I'd like you to discuss that question further. Also, discuss how you got your names—and compare that with the four ways we studied today.

Coaching Tips

[1] Note-taking and Listening: Organization
Often, in the introduction of a lecture, the speaker uses signal words or phrases to tell you how the lecture will be organized. How many parts will this lecture have? What words does the speaker use to give you this information? She says that the lecture will be divided into two halves. To show the two parts in your notes, you could divide the page vertically, or horizontally, like this: [see video for note-taking example].

Find audioscript for the other Coaching Tips at www.pearsonlongman.com/contemporarytopics

Talk about the Topic *page 8*

Manny: It's off-track but . . .

Mia: Anyway, why don't we start by telling how we each got our names? I'll go first. Mia was just a name my parents liked. Pretty simple!

Manny: Well, in my case, I got my name from the first way that the lecturer mentioned, which was custom. My father was named Manny and my grandfather was also.

Hannah: Well, with me—Hannah—I was named after my mom's high school teacher. I guess my mom really admired this woman.

Mia: What about you, River?

River: Uhmm, I'm not really sure where my name comes from. I doubt my parents chose it to help me socially. I mean, *River* isn't exactly a popular name!

Hannah: Well, maybe they wanted you to, you know, get noticed?

River: Oh, I get noticed, for sure. Every time I tell someone my name, they stop for a second and look at me strangely.

Mia: So you must think names really do matter?

River: Yeah. Hey, do you think I got a low score on my last test because of my name?

Hannah: Seriously though, this lecture's made me realize it's a big responsibility for a parent to choose, for their kids. Don't you think?

Mia: You mean, it's the parents' responsibility to give good names?

Hannah: Yeah, right.

River: Yeah, that's exactly why, if I had children, I would give them a classic name, like *John* or *Jennifer*.

Manny: Not me. My kid's going to be the next *Shakira* or *Tiger Woods*—someone unforgettable!

Take the Unit Test

1. What is the main focus of the lecture?
2. Passing a name from one generation to the next is an example of what?
3. Hannah was named after her mom's favorite teacher. What is this an example of?
4. What is the most common reason parents choose a particular name?
5. What is one social benefit that a name can provide?
6. What's the definition of a "classic" name?
7. Does the lecturer think that it's beneficial to have a classic name?
8. What does it mean to associate stereotypes with names?
9. Why did the researchers give the teachers the same homework assignment?
10. What did the homework assignment research show?

Extend the Topic *page 10*

Reporter: So, can you tell our listeners your name?

Auriel: Sure. It's Auriel. Auriel Whitaker.

Reporter: Auriel, huh? So, do you know how your parents decided on your name?

Auriel: Yeah. I was born when the movie *The Little Mermaid* first came out. So a lot of baby girls were named *Ariel* after that. In the movie, Ariel is strong and independent. My mom said they admired how she knew what she wanted. So, I guess they wanted me to be like her . . . or maybe they just wanted me to be a good swimmer, you know, a little mermaid. But actually, my name is *Auriel*, with a *u* after the *a*—my parents liked the sound of that a little better.

Reporter: What about you—do you like the sound of it? Would you ever change your name?

Auriel: Uh, well, it doesn't really matter. I mean, my friends and everyone actually call me A. J. *Jenna* is my middle name.

Reporter: I see. So you have a nickname . . .

ANSWER KEY

Build Your Vocabulary *pages 3–4*

B. 1. classic 2. symbol 3. gender 4. prime
5. assignments 6. discrimination 7. custom
8. image 9. generations 10. admire **C. Interact
with Vocabulary!** 1. of 2. by 3. after 4. as 5. to
6. with 7. to 8. down 9. on 10. out of

Focus Your Attention *page 5*

A. Signal phrases: Today's lecture will be divided
into two parts. In the first half, . . .; in the second
half, we'll focus in on . . . Topics: an overview of
sociological research; gender in the workplace

Listen for Main Ideas *pages 6–7*

B. 1. a 2. c 3. b 4. c 5. a

Listen for Details *page 7*

B. 1. T 2. T 3. F (father) 4. T 5. T 6. F (*Anna*
not *Alex*) 7. T 8. F (half of the assignments) 9. T
10. F (name him *Michael,* not *Hubert*)

Talk about the Topic *page 8*

A. 1. Mia 2. Manny 3. Hannah 4. River
B. 1. Asking for clarification or confirmation
2. Asking for opinions or ideas 3. Asking for
clarification or confirmation

Review Your Notes *page 9*

Name:	Ex. of:
Alex/Alexandra/Dr. Shaw	how different names change what we think of people
Sarah	relying on custom (ex. naming after a grandmother)
Robert or Anna	classic/because it's likeable
Darvlin	unusual, to get noticed
Taylor	gender-neutral, to avoid gender discrimination
Hubert	how a name can carry a stereotype (ex. graded paper example v. *Michael*)

Take the Unit Test

1. c 2. b 3. d 4. c 5. c 6. a 7. d 8. d 9. b 10. a

SOCIOLOGY: Names

 Listen to each question. Circle the letter of the correct answer.

1. a. why names are important

b. why we all have names

c. how parents choose names

d. how names have different meanings

2. a. relying on stereotypes

b. relying on custom

c. relying on meaning

d. relying on sound or feeling

3. a. choosing a classic name

b. choosing a father's name

c. choosing a grandmother's name

d. choosing the name of someone the parent admired

4. a. because they think about the social benefits of the name

b. because they prefer classic names

c. because they like the name

d. because they want to follow a custom

5. a. People change their names because of you.

b. People stereotype you because of your name.

c. People notice you because of your name.

d. People name their children after you.

6. a. a name that never goes out of style

b. a name that has a nice feeling

c. a name that gives someone an advantage

d. a name that has a beautiful sound

7. a. Yes, she does.

b. No, she doesn't.

c. She doesn't say.

d. She can't say for sure.

8. a. to judge people by their names

b. to hear a name and "see" an image

c. to decide what a person is like from his or her name

d. all of the above

9. a. to make it easy to grade

b. to make the name the only factor

c. to make it faster to grade

d. to make the teachers happy

10. a. how people hold stereotypes about certain names

b. how teachers are unfair

c. how a name like *Michael* can make you smarter

d. none of the above

LINGUISTICS
Global English

TEACHING TIPS

UNIT OVERVIEW

In this unit, students will explore what it means for English to be a global language. The lecture focuses on two contrasting views of English and its future use around the world. Follow-up projects extend the topic to a listening and a discussion about varieties and pronunciation of English; a reading about students from non-English-speaking countries studying business courses in English; and a research project on varieties of English.

Connect to the Topic *page 12*   *~10 minutes*

Students answer questions about using English. Questions focus on students' individual needs for English, as well as their opinions on why English has become the current *lingua franca* of the world. Students are also introduced to the term *global economy*.

Build Your Vocabulary *pages 13–14*   *~15 minutes*

Students study these words and phrases related to linguistics and the global use of English:

acknowledge	global (language)	proficient (in)
at work	hold on to	replaced by
authority on	instead of	required for
communicate	international standard	retained (their ability)
domains	nevertheless	supported by
facilitate	official (language)	unprecedented
(communication)	points of view	

For the Interact with Vocabulary! activity, you may want to encourage students to first notice the boldfaced words. Figuring out these collocations can help students more quickly unscramble the sentences.

BONUS ACTIVITY

Consider having students work in pairs to do a vocabulary expansion activity in which they use their dictionaries to look up related forms of the target vocabulary—for example, *acknowledgment* or *proficiency.*

Focus Your Attention *page 15*   *~10 minutes*

Students learn cues that lecturers use when focusing on comparing ideas. They learn how to organize their notes based on these cues:

*Today you'll hear **two contrasting points of view** about . . .*
*This afternoon we'll **compare** . . .*
*We'll look at some of **the differences between** . . .*

You may want to explain that in the example, the numbers *1, 2,* and *3* are meant to show how a student has organized her notes in advance, anticipating arguments the speaker will give.

Listen to the Lecture *pages 16–17* ~30 minutes

Prior to listening to the unit lecture, students write their own ideas about the future role of English as the *lingua franca* (Before You Listen). Then students listen to the lecture and answer multiple-choice questions (Listen for Main Ideas) and true/false questions (Listen for Details).

Lecture video time: 6 min. 19 sec.   *Number of episodes: 8*

> **NOTE**
>
> Remember that with the DVD, you can play the lecture in different modes: video, video with subtitles, video with Coaching Tips, video with Presentation Points, video with Coaching Tips and subtitles, and video with Coaching Tips and Presentation Points. (We do not recommend playing the video with both the Presentation Points and subtitles on.) Note that while the DVD is compatible with most computer media players, for optimum viewing we suggest playing the DVD on a television using a DVD player. You can also play the lecture as audio only, using the CD.

Talk about the Topic *page 18* ~20 minutes

Four students—Michael, May, Yhinny, and Qiang—discuss the lecture. Part A focuses on matching these students with comments from the discussion. In Part B, your students work on these discussion strategies:

- Agreeing: "Oh, definitely."
- Disagreeing: "You're joking, right?"

For Part C, students are encouraged to use the discussion strategies they've learned. They may use phrases from the student discussion and/or the Discussion Strategy box, or they may come up with their own.

Student discussion video time: 1 min. 28 sec.

Review Your Notes *page 19* ~15 minutes

Students work with a partner to paraphrase the main ideas from the lecture. Then they use their notes to complete an outline of the lecture.

Take the Unit Test *Teacher's Pack page 13* ~15 minutes

You may want to play the lecture again just before giving the test. Students answer standard test questions about the content of the lecture. Specifically, the test covers the following: the definition of English as a global language, two points of view on the use of English globally, examples of contexts in which English is used, and the lecturer's point of view on the future use of English globally.

Extend the Topic *pages 20–21* ~30 minutes

- Listening and Discussion: Students hear a speaker at an international forum present a talk on varieties of English. Then they discuss two questions about the talk.
- Reading and Discussion: Students learn about and discuss the push by many of the world's top business schools to teach required classes in English.
- Research and Presentation: Students conduct additional research on varieties of English or related areas of interest. For example, students might enjoy comparing the English slang used in their respective home countries.

Focus Your Attention:
Try It Out! *page 15*

Speaker: Today I want to give you two contrasting points of view about varieties of English. There are many varieties of English now, Korean English, Indian English, American English, and so on. Some people are worried that there are too many varieties. They say this is going to cause big communication problems as English is used more throughout the world. There's another way to think about this, though. That is to say, yes, there are many varieties of English, but this isn't a serious problem. Here are some reasons why I say this. The first reason is that the basic grammar is still the same whether the English is spoken in China, or Australia, or Brazil, or the United States. The second reason is, yes, some vocabulary is different. But most words are the same, right? . . .

Listen for Main Ideas and Listen
for Details *pages 16–17*

Linguistics lecturer: E1 All right, today's topic is English as a "global language." Now, linguists use the term "global language" to refer to the use of English worldwide for global communication. I know some of you, your first languages are Spanish or Chinese, but English is our common language here in the classroom; what's known as *the lingua franca*. It's the common language throughout the world right now as well, isn't it? Professor Braj B. Kachru, an authority on the use of English, called the current global use of English "unprecedented." This means that in the history of the world there has never been one language used by so many people. It just hasn't happened before. And it's important that we, as linguists, consider what it means for English to be a "global language." E2 Now, today, I'm going to give you two contrasting points of view about English as a global language. One is that English is now used all over the world, and it's actually replacing other languages. Now, according to this point of view, English will be used instead of other languages in the future. Eventually, so this argument goes, it will be the only language people speak. Now, the second point of view is that English will not truly become a global language and replace other languages because it's not the main language spoken by people worldwide in their daily lives. Supporters of this point of view acknowledge that people all over the world use English every day to communicate in certain domains, like business, or science, or government. They contend, however, that

people have retained their first languages, and will continue to do so. Now, this point of view is supported by linguist David Crystal, author of *English as a Global Language* and other books. E3 So let's examine some facts that support the first point of view. Now, first, English is clearly the dominant language of business, science, and international travel. When we need a common language, whether in airports or hotels or at international meetings, it's English. If you take a taxi in Rome and you don't speak Italian, the driver is more likely to use English than another language, right? Now, in addition, the European Union uses English for both written and spoken communication. Scientists worldwide use English. Business schools in Europe are now teaching their classes in English—even in France, a country that has fought very hard in the past to keep English out. I'm sure all of you can think of many situations where English is the common language; how about the Internet? You use English there, don't you? E4 Second, seventy-five countries use English as an official language in the government and in banks, and so on. Now, for some countries, like England, English is the only official language. In other countries, like India, there's more than one official language. In India, Hindi and English are both official languages used to run the country. So, to sum up: We know millions of people throughout the world need a common language to facilitate communication. That's clear. Right now, being proficient in English gives them an advantage in many situations. Nevertheless, does this mean that English will eventually replace other languages? E5 With that question in mind, let's turn to the second point of view: why some people don't think English will replace other languages. Now, first, according to recent data, more than a billion people speak some English as a second or third language. However, English isn't their primary language at home and with friends. Now this is a key point: These people may use English for work or school each day, but nowhere else. All right. Even in English-speaking countries, millions of people prefer to speak a language other than English all the time. For example, Spanish is very common in large cities like New York or L.A. E6 Second, I mentioned there are seventy-five countries where English is the official language, but this doesn't mean that everyone there speaks English. Not at all. Take India, again. Most sources agree that less than half of the population actually knows some English. OK. Third, people may only know the English required for specific job situations. For example, the taxi driver in Rome that I mentioned earlier may only know phrases like "Where are you going?" or "What is the name of your hotel?" And another example is with the airlines. Pilots in Korea or China may only learn the English they need on the job. English doesn't replace Korean or Chinese for them. They don't use English instead of their first language. They use it in addition to. There are many situations worldwide like this, aren't there? It's evident that millions of people worldwide know only the English required for specific situations. English isn't their main language in daily life. E7 So, where does that leave us? Well, now that you've heard the reasons behind these two points of view about English as a global language, what do you think? Myself, I don't see it replacing other languages. I agree with David Crystal that language is a part of culture. As globalization continues, the use of English spreads, people will want to hold on to their own languages and cultures more than ever. Do you agree? E8 I want you to think about these questions: First: With English as a global language, do we need an international standard—a form that we all agree on? Question 2: If yes, which standard should we use? Or—last question—is it OK to have different varieties of English, like Italian-English or Japanese-English? And why? Think these over, and we'll see you next time.

Coaching Tips

[1] Note-taking: Noting contrasts How will the lecturer present the topic of global English? He says that he'll "give you two contrasting points of view." From this you know that you'll be noting contrasts, or differences, between two views. Consider creating two columns for your notes, one for each view. Or, you could draw a line across the middle of your paper and write one view at the top of the paper and the other at the bottom. Separating the views like this will help you quickly recognize the two views.

Find audioscript for the other Coaching Tips at www.pearsonlongman.com/contemporarytopics.

Talk about the Topic *page 18*

Yhinny: Hey, you know when the lecturer was talking about languages and culture?

Qiang: Yeah.

Michael: Yeah.

Yhinny: And he said other languages will exist as long as other cultures exist?

Michael: Yeah.

Yhinny: Well, I'm in total agreement with him. I don't think English will ever replace other languages.

May: Oh, definitely.

Qiang: Right! I don't see other languages disappearing. I mean, yeah, I need English for class now, or maybe someday at my job. But when I call my parents or my friends back home in China, we don't use English.

May: Oh, it's the same with me. I have so many Jordanian friends who speak English, but when we're together, we only speak Arabic.

Michael: Well, what about the idea of having an international standard for English? I mean, do you guys think we need one?

Qiang: What exactly do they mean by "international standard"?

May: It's like a set of rules . . .

Michael: Right.

May: . . . for grammar, spelling, I don't know, pronunciation—that everyone agrees to.

Qiang: Well, how's everyone going to agree to it? It seems kind of impossible.

Yhinny: Well, it seems likely to me that there'll always be varieties—kind of like dialects—of English as you go to different places around the world.

May: Uh-huh.

Qiang: Yeah, so a standard wouldn't be helpful, would it?

Michael: But, I mean, if you don't have a standard, then you're going to start getting all kinds of crazy vocabulary words and weird spellings.

May: You're joking, right? English already has crazy vocab words and weird spellings!

Yhinny: I know.

Qiang: That's exactly how I feel.

Yhinny: It's crazy.

Michael: Yeah.

Take the Unit Test

1. How do linguists describe a "global language"?
2. What does it mean that the global use of English is "unprecedented"?
3. Which best describes the first point of view about global English?
4. What does the example of an Italian taxi driver using English demonstrate?
5. Why does the speaker mention business schools in France?
6. What does the second point of view say about global English?
7. More than one billion people speak some English, the lecturer says. He then adds a "key point" about those English speakers. What is it?
8. What does the speaker say about a country's official language?
9. What is the use of English by Korean and Chinese pilots an example of?
10. Does the speaker agree with David Crystal's point of view?

Extend the Topic *page 20*

Speaker: Between 300 and 400 million people speak English as their first language. And many millions more speak it as a second or third language. It's estimated that one out of every five people in the world is competent in English. Soon, the number of people who speak English as a first language will be less than the number of people who speak it as a second or third language. Specifically, a lot of business communication is now among people who don't speak English as a first language. This raises some important questions. For example, should there be an international standard for English? If so, which variety should it be based on? If not, which variety of English should students learn? And, which pronunciation of English should be used? These are just a few of the questions I'll be addressing today . . .

ANSWER KEY

Build Your Vocabulary *pages 13–14*

B. 1. accept as true 2. share information 3. areas or fields 4. help make happen 5. worldwide 6. although true 7. approved by an authority 8. skillful 9. kept 10. never happened before
C. Interact with Vocabulary! 1. is an authority on 2. will English be used instead of 3. two contrasting points of view 4. was proficient in four other languages 5. is supported by many linguists 6. be replaced by English 7. many people use English at work 8. want to hold on to 9. that we need an international standard 10. the English required for

Focus Your Attention *page 15*

A. Two contrasting points of view on varieties of English: 1. There are too many varieties; this will cause big problems. 2. It's not a serious problem because basic grammar and vocabulary are still the same.

Listen for Main Ideas *pages 16–17*

B. 1. b 2. b 3. b 4. b 5. a

Listen for Details *page 17*

B. 1. T 2. F (will replace) 3. F (isn't the main language) 4. F (are now starting to teach in English) 5. F (as their second or third language) 6. T 7. F (don't speak English at home) 8. T 9. T 10. F (asks if there should be an international standard)

Talk about the Topic *page 18*

A. 1. Yhinny 2. Qiang 3. Michael 4. May
B. 1. Agreeing 2. Agreeing 3. Agreeing 4. Disagreeing

Review Your Notes *page 19*

I. a language used worldwide for global communication; *lingua franca* (common language) in international situations; **II.** English will replace other languages; it will become only language people speak; A. English is the dominant language of business, science, international travel (EU, business schools in Europe use English); B. English use on the Internet is worldwide; C. 75 countries use English as official language; **III.** English won't replace other languages; A. More than a billion people speak English as a 2nd or 3rd language, but it isn't their primary language; B. In countries where English is official language, not everyone speaks it, e.g. India; C. People may only know the English required for their job; **IV.** Answers will vary.

Take the Unit Test

1. d 2. c 3. a 4. c 5. a 6. d 7. a 8. c 9. d 10. b

UNIT 2 TEST — LINGUISTICS: Global English

 Listen to each question. Circle the letter of the correct answer.

1. a. as a language that's difficult to learn
   b. as a language that's used in seventy-five countries
   c. as a language that people like to study
   d. as a language that's used for worldwide communication

2. a. that its use is widespread
   b. that its use is common
   c. that its use is greater now than at any time in history
   d. that its use is huge

3. a. English is used all over; it's replacing other languages.
   b. English is used at work only.
   c. English is used as a second language.
   d. English is the only language people should speak.

4. a. that Italians like English
   b. that taxi drivers in Italy are friendly
   c. that there's a need for a common language
   d. that people prefer to speak a language other than English

5. a. to show how important English is becoming
   b. to show that French people like English
   c. to show that French people study English
   d. to show that English is an official language

6. a. that it's not the main language spoken around the world in daily life
   b. that it's used only in certain domains
   c. that it's not going to be the only language used in the future
   d. all of the above

7. a. that many of them use English for work or school, but nowhere else
   b. that English is now their primary language
   c. that many of them use English for communication at home
   d. that many of them use English for communication with friends

8. a. that it's spoken by everyone in that country
   b. that it's used only by government officials
   c. that it's not necessarily spoken by everyone within that country
   d. that it's studied by everyone in that country

9. a. English not replacing a first language
   b. English being used at work
   c. English being used in addition to a first language
   d. all of the above

10. a. No, he doesn't.
    b. Yes, he does.
    c. He doesn't say.
    d. It isn't clear.

TEACHING TIPS

UNIT OVERVIEW

In this unit, students will work with different concepts related to phobias and the treatment of this psychological condition. The lecture focuses on the definition of the term *phobias*, types of phobias, causes of phobias, and treatments of phobias. Follow-up projects extend the topic to a listening, a reading, and a research project related to mental health issues.

Connect to the Topic *page 22*   *~10 minutes*

Students are exposed to the term *phobias*, as well as the names of two specific phobias: *acrophobia* (a fear of heights) and *arachnophobia* (a fear of spiders). They then take a survey about their beliefs concerning fears and phobias. Students share their responses with a partner.

Build Your Vocabulary *pages 23–24*   *~15 minutes*

Students study these words and phrases related to psychology and phobias:

afraid of
(human) behavior
(common)
   characteristic
classified (into
   categories)
classified by
constant

definition of
developed (a phobia)
duration
physical (response)
psychologist
rational
reaction to

run in families
sign of
theories on
topic in
(childhood) trauma
treatments for
type of

After the Interact with Vocabulary! activity, you may want to have students practice using the boldfaced words with their partners. Knowing collocations can help students expand their vocabularies and increase their fluency.

Focus Your Attention *page 25*   *~10 minutes*

Students learn speech cues that lecturers use when focusing on key words. They learn how to organize their notes based on these cues from the speaker:

Pausing
Slowing down
Speaking more loudly

Repeating the key
   word
Spelling the key word

Defining the key word
using an introductory
phrase

Listen to the Lecture *pages 26–27*   *~30 minutes*

Before listening to the unit lecture, students consider why some people develop phobias (Before You Listen). Then students listen to the lecture and identify true statements (Listen for Main Ideas) and answer multiple-choice questions (Listen for Details).
Lecture video time: 7 min. 45 sec.   *Number of episodes: 9*

> **NOTE**
>
> Remember that with the DVD, you can play the lecture in different modes: video, video with subtitles, video with Coaching Tips, video with Presentation Points, video with Coaching Tips and subtitles, and video with Coaching Tips and Presentation Points. (We do not recommend playing the video with both the Presentation Points and subtitles on.) Note that while the DVD is compatible with most computer media players, for optimum viewing we suggest playing the DVD on a television using a DVD player. You can also play the lecture as audio only, using the CD.

Talk about the Topic *page 28*   *~20 minutes*

Four students—Alana, Ayman, Molly, and Rob—discuss the lecture. Part A focuses on matching these students with comments from the discussion. In Part B, your students work on identifying these discussion strategies:

- Offering a fact or example: "I was hiking last summer . . . "
- Asking for clarification or confirmation: "What does that mean . . . ?"
- Keeping the discussion on topic: "Seriously guys . . . let's stay focused, OK?"

For Part C, students are encouraged to use the discussion strategies they've learned. They may use phrases from the student discussion and/or the Discussion Strategy box, or they may come up with their own. Keep in mind that some students may be reluctant to talk about their fears, while others may be very open about discussing them.
Student discussion video time: 1 min. 43 sec.

Review Your Notes *page 29*   *~15 minutes*

Students focus on reconstructing their notes, paying attention to key words and phrases.

> **BONUS ACTIVITY**
>
> Have pairs form small groups to exchange ideas and complete their notes together.

Take the Unit Test *Teacher's Pack page 19*   *~15 minutes*

You may want to play the lecture again just before giving the test. Students answer standard test questions about the content of the lecture. Specifically, the test covers the following: definition of the term *phobia*, examples of common phobias, characteristics of phobias, and theories about phobias.

Extend the Topic *pages 30–31*   *~30 minutes*

- Listening and Discussion: Students listen to a TV talk show guest share her phobia. Then they discuss what they heard.
- Reading and Discussion: Students read about and discuss three different approaches to treating phobias.
- Research and Presentation: Students research a phobia that interests them and then compare and present their findings.

AUDIOSCRIPT

Focus Your Attention: Try It Out! *page 25*

Speaker: Psychology is the study of human behavior. There are several branches of psychology. One major branch is called *clinical* psychology. That's *clinical* psychology: c-l-i-n-i-c-a-l. Clinical psychology is the study of mental and emotional problems. One important example of a mental or emotional problem is a *phobia* . . . a *phobia*. . . . Today, let's look at the two main types of phobias . . .

Listen for Main Ideas and Listen for Details *pages 26–27*

Psychology lecturer: **E1** Hello everyone. Today, we're going to study an interesting topic in psychology: phobias. We'll first learn about types of phobias, and then the causes of phobias and the treatment of phobias. **E2** But first, let's get the definition clear. A phobia is a fear, yes, but a phobia isn't a normal fear; it's an extreme fear. It's basically a very strong, very focused fear. There are two main kinds of phobias. One is a specific phobia, like the fear of a dog, and the second type is a situational phobia, like the fear of public speaking. An important thing to remember: We all have some fears; that's natural. But a phobia is much stronger. OK. Sometimes it can be so constant or it can be so serious that it interferes with a person's life. Then some kind of treatment may be necessary. **E3** For example, one of my clients—I'll call her Maria— she used to have a phobia of elevators. So, a situational phobia. She couldn't ride in an elevator without being terrified. Sometimes she would panic and start breathing fast as soon as she got into an elevator. After a while, she refused to ride in any elevators at all. Even if she had to walk up twenty flights of stairs, she would do just that—in order to avoid being in an elevator. Her life was changed by the phobia. **E4** All right. So we have a basic definition of a phobia: an extreme fear, and one that interferes with the person's life. OK, now let's go a little deeper into our definition of phobia here. Psychologists have come up with three characteristics of a phobia. These characteristics help us to understand the difference between a phobia and a normal fear. First, a phobia isn't a rational response. It's a very strong reaction, too strong for the situation. For my patient Maria, who was afraid of elevators, this meant that she had a very strong physical reaction if someone even asked her to get onto an elevator. She'd start sweating and shaking—not a rational response. The second characteristic is this: The duration is long. A phobia often lasts for a long time. It may last several years, or even a person's whole life. And third, the reaction is too strong for the person to control. For example, for Maria, even though when she told herself not to be afraid to ride in the elevator, it didn't help. She still felt very scared no matter what she did. Her fear was uncontrollable. OK, so those are the three characteristics of a phobia. It's an irrational response, it's long-lasting, and it's uncontrollable. **E5** Now, let's spend a minute going over some types of common phobias. It's important to understand that phobias are classified by the thing or situation that the person fears. Greek or Latin names are usually used to describe the fear. So here are some examples: *hypno*, h-y-p-n-o, means "sleep," so fear of sleep is *hypno*phobia. *Cyno*, c-y-n-o, means "dog." So a fear of dogs is *cyno*phobia. Maria's phobia is known as *claustro*phobia—a fear of being in closed places. That's c-l-a-u-s-t-r-o. A very common phobia, I might add. **E6** Now to the causes of phobias. One theory is that a phobia is learned. This means that something happens that causes somebody to feel afraid. For example, someone could have learned to be afraid of dogs if he were attacked and injured by a dog as a child. This is an example of direct learning. People can also learn to have phobias indirectly by watching how other people react. For example, let's imagine a young man—we'll call him David. David's mother had always been afraid of dogs. Whenever David and his mother were together and they saw a dog, his mother would get very scared, even panicked. When David saw how his mother reacted, he became very scared, too. He developed this same phobia, cynophobia, from watching his mother. In fact, psychologists find that phobias tend to run in families—that is, they tend to be learned in the same way among family members. **E7** The second theory about how phobias develop is the association theory. The theory says that a phobia is usually the result of a trauma, or difficult experience that occurred in childhood. In other words, an adult associates a particular object or situation with a past trauma. For example, one of my patients was very afraid of the dark. After some therapy sessions, we discovered that his father used to put him in a closet as punishment when he was young. Now this man associates being in the dark with this terrible childhood experience. So those are the two theories—one, that a phobia can be learned, and two, that a phobia is caused by an association with an unpleasant memory or event from our past. **E8** Well, there's hope here. We have treatments for phobias. And what do you think these treatments are? Well, first, psychologists know that if a phobia has been learned, it can usually be unlearned. In other words, a person can learn how to change a certain behavior. This "unlearning" is usually done step-by-step, so that a person will gradually lose their deep fear. And, second, if a phobia's a sign of a deeper psychological problem, then the psychologist can help the patient to become aware of this deeper problem. That awareness can lead to getting rid of the phobia for good. **E9** Well, that's enough for now. Are there any questions? Any questions at all?

Coaching Tips

[1] Note-taking: Noting definitions At this point, what do you know about the term *phobia*? The topic of this lecture is phobias, so getting a complete definition and full understanding of the term will be important. Your definition might look something like this: [see video for note-taking example]. Always try to leave a little space around a key word and definition. You never know when a lecturer might add a little more information!

Find audioscript for the other Coaching Tips at www.pearsonlongman.com/contemporarytopics.

Talk about the Topic *page 28*

Ayman: So, do we all understand what a phobia is?

Alana: I do. I have a phobia of lectures in English.

Ayman: Seriously, guys. We don't have much time, let's stay focused, OK?

Alana: OK.

Ayman: So, anyone has an example of regular phobia?

Molly: Well, I don't know if it's a phobia, but I hate spiders. I'm completely terrified of them.

Rob: I'm the same way with snakes.

Molly: Oh yeah?

Rob: Oh yeah. I was hiking last summer and I almost stepped on one. Oh, it got me so scared, I was screaming.

Alana: Well, but those are natural reactions, don't you think? I mean, spiders and snakes can be dangerous. So, those fears seem normal to me—but not extreme.

Ayman: You know the "uncontrollable" part of the definition made me think of my friend back . . .

Alana: Wait, wait. What does that mean, "uncontrollable"?

Rob: Oh. Un-control-able. So, something that you can't control.

Alana: Oh.

Rob: Yeah?

Alana: OK, yeah.

Ayman: Anyway, that part of the definition made me think of my friend back in Dubai. You know she, she wouldn't use these revolving doors—you know, at store entrances?

Rob: Really?

Ayman: Yeah.

Rob: Well, why?

Ayman: I don't know—I guess it has something to do with closed spaces fear? What do you call it?

Alana: Claustrophobia.

Molly: Uh-huh.

Rob: Oh yeah.

Ayman: Yeah. So we'd go to the mall if—if, if there was a revolving door she wouldn't go in. She would just stand outside and wait for me.

Molly: Huh. Has she thought of going to therapy for it? . . . What?

Ayman: Well, back home we don't believe in getting therapy for these kind(s) of problems.

Rob: You see?

Ayman: But, but I wish she'd get over it because I'm tired of shopping alone!

Rob: That's strange!

Take the Unit Test

1. Which is the best definition of a phobia?
2. What is the fear of public speaking an example of?
3. What are the three characteristics of a phobia?
4. What do psychologists call a fear of sleeping?
5. What would someone with hypnophobia most likely do?
6. How can a phobia be directly learned? Choose *two* answers.
7. The association theory says a phobia is usually a result of which situation?
8. Which is true of all phobias?
9. Which word best describes the speaker's attitude about phobia treatments?
10. What's the speaker's main point?

Extend the Topic *page 30*

Host: Thank you. We're back and speaking with our guest, Stephanie. So, Stephanie, you told our producers that you used to have some kind of phobia.

Stephanie: Yeah, I used to be so totally afraid of heights. Crazy afraid. It's called acrophobia. If I had to stand on a high ladder, or go in a tall building, I, . . . well, it was awful.

Host: What would happen? Can you talk about it?

Stephanie: Well, as soon as I got up high, my heart would start beating really fast. I'd have trouble breathing, I'd get so scared. I'd feel sick. The worst was when I was driving over a high bridge. I wanted to just stop driving. Just get out of my car and get off the bridge! I'd panic.

Host: So what would you do? I mean, you can't avoid bridges when you're driving, right?

Stephanie: No, you can't. Right. So, I went to a doctor. She knew a good treatment. It's worked for me. I mean, I still get a little nervous, but at least I can drive to work now!

Host: Well that's great. . . . Isn't that great everyone?

ANSWER KEY

Build Your Vocabulary *pages 23–24*
B. 1. actions 2. features 3. grouped 4. continuous 5. began to have 6. length of time 7. related to the body 8. person who treats mental problems 9. reasonable 10. bad experience **C. Interact with Vocabulary!** 1. by 2. of 3. on 4. in 5. of 6. of 7. to 8. in 9. for 10. of

Focus Your Attention *page 25*
A. Cues: pausing, slowing down, speaking more loudly, repeating key word, spelling out and defining key words; Key words: clinical psychology, phobia

Listen for Main Ideas *page 26*
B. Students should check items 2, 3, 4, and 5. The others are false for the following reasons: 1. (does interfere) 6. (anyone can have) 7. (two: learned and association) 8. (can)

Listen for Details *pages 26–27*
B. 1. b 2. c 3. b 4. a 5. b 6. c 7. b 8. c

Talk about the Topic *page 28*
A. 1. Molly 2. Alana 3. Rob 4. Ayman
B. 1. Keeping the discussion on topic 2. Offering a fact or example 3. Asking for clarification or confirmation 4. Offering a fact or example

Review Your Notes *page 29*
Def. of a phobia: An extreme/strong/focused fear; **Main kinds of phobias:** 1. specific Ex.: fear of dogs 2. situational Ex.: fear of public speaking; **Characteristics of a phobia:** 1. irrational 2. long lasting 3. uncontrollable; **Classification system of phobias:** Latin/Greek; **Ex.'s of names of phobias:** hypno/cyno/claustro; **2 theories on causes of phobias:** 1. learned (direct/indirect) 2. association

Take the Unit Test
1. c 2. b 3. d 4. a 5. b 6. a and b 7. b 8. c 9. a 10. b

 **TEST PSYCHOLOGY: Phobias**

 Listen to each question. Circle the letter of the correct answer.

1. a. a temporary feeling

b. a way of avoiding a situation

c. a strong, focused fear

d. a mild, occasional sensation

2. a. a specific phobia

b. a situational phobia

c. a psychological theory

d. a characteristic of a phobia

3. a. rational, extreme, difficult to control

b. reasonable, violent, easy to control

c. temporary, mild, able to be controlled

d. not rational, long lasting, uncontrollable

4. a. hypnophobia

b. cynophobia

c. claustrophobia

d. heliophobia

5. a. enjoy going to bed

b. try to stay awake

c. stay away from dogs

d. stay inside during daylight hours

6. a. by being injured

b. by being attacked

c. by seeing something terrible

d. by hearing about something terrible

7. a. a dog bite

b. a childhood trauma

c. fear of sleep

d. fear of elevators

8. a. They can be unlearned.

b. They can be cured for good.

c. They can be treated.

d. all of the above

9. a. hopeful

b. doubtful

c. neutral

d. angry

10. a. that having fears and phobias is normal

b. that having a phobia is serious but treatable

c. that psychologists still don't know a lot about phobias

d. that better medications are needed for people with phobias

TEACHING TIPS

UNIT OVERVIEW

In this unit, students will explore factors that contribute to the success of a restaurant. The lecture focuses on contrast—namely, the various ways a restaurant staff must work hard so that customers can do the opposite: relax. Follow-up projects extend the topic to hearing about a waiter's experience, designing a menu, and researching related professions.

Connect to the Topic *page 32*   *~10 minutes*

Students answer the research question "What's important to you when you go to a restaurant?" Then they read customers' responses. In pairs, students compare their own responses with those of the customers. The terms *go out of business, atmosphere*, and *waitstaff* are introduced.

Build Your Vocabulary *pages 33–34*   *~15 minutes*

Students study these words and phrases related to culinary arts and owning a restaurant.

ambience	contribute to	opposite
balance	create for	(at the) outset
bring enjoyment to	emphasized	perspective
people	factors in	a reservation for
built on	guarantee (success)	dinner
components	known for	satisfied with
content with	looking forward to	success of
contrast		

After the Interact with Vocabulary! activity, you may want to have students practice using the boldfaced words with their partners. Knowing collocations can help students expand their vocabularies and increase their fluency.

Focus Your Attention *page 35*   *~10 minutes*

Students learn cues that lecturers use when focusing on main topics and subtopics. They learn how to organize notes by writing the topic and then indenting the subtopics.

Today we're going to talk about . . . (main topic)   *This afternoon I'm going to discuss . . . (main topic)*
I want to focus first on . . . (subtopic)   *Specifically, we'll look at two aspects . . . (subtopic)*
Then I plan to consider . . . (subtopic)

Listen to the Lecture *pages 36–37*   *~30 minutes*

Prior to listening to the unit lecture, students write their own ideas about the key to a restaurant's success (Before Your Listen). Then they listen to the lecture, answer multiple-choice questions (Listen for Main Ideas), and use their notes to complete statements (Listen for Details).
Lecture video time: 7 min. 13 sec.   *Number of episodes: 10*

Talk about the Topic *page 38*

~20 minutes

Four students—Hannah, River, Mia, and Manny—discuss the lecture. Part A focuses on matching these students with ideas from the discussion. In Part B, your students work on identifying these discussion strategies:

- Agreeing: "OK. I can see that . . . "
- Asking for clarification or confirmation: "Can anyone explain it to me?"
- Paraphrasing: "I think he means that if you run a restaurant . . . "

For Part C, students are encouraged to use the discussion strategies they've learned. They may use phrases from the student discussion and/or the Discussion Strategy box, or they may come up with their own.
Student discussion video time: 1 min. 37 sec.

Review Your Notes *page 39*

~15 minutes

Students work with a partner to reconstruct the main ideas from the lecture, focusing on topics and subtopics.

BONUS ACTIVITY

As a consolidation activity, have students do a role play based on the information in the lecture—for example, the manager or chef talking to the staff prior to opening, or Kate and Justin interacting with the waitstaff.

Take the Unit Test *Teacher's Pack page 25*

~15 minutes

You may want to play the lecture again just before giving the test. Students answer standard test questions about the content of the lecture. Specifically, the test covers the following: key reasons that a restaurant succeeds, why independent restaurants fail, essential factors in a good dining experience, and meeting customer expectations.

Extend the Topic *pages 40–41*

~30 minutes

- Listening and Discussion: Students hear about a waiter's experiences with customers. Then they discuss related ideas.
- Reading and Discussion: Students consider the importance of menu design.
- Research and Presentation: Students research and present on professions related to culinary arts—for example, food photography or restaurant design.

Focus Your Attention:
Try It Out! *page 35*

Speaker: Good afternoon. Today we're going to talk about the waitstaff in a restaurant. First I want to focus on who makes up the staff. Who these people are. What they're called. For example, the chefs, the cooks, the servers, and so on. Then I plan to talk about what their roles and responsibilities are. This will help you understand how they all work together, and depend on each other to make the restaurant successful. All right, so now let's get started. Let's look at who works in, say, a medium-size restaurant.

Listen for Main Ideas and Listen for Details *pages 36–37*

Culinary arts lecturer: E1 Good afternoon. Today, we're going to discuss how creating a positive dining experience is key to the success of your restaurant. A smart restaurant owner needs to understand two major concepts about customer service: First, that there are many factors that contribute to making customers feel satisfied. And second, that a successful dining experience is built on contrast. Now what do I mean by "contrast"? By this I mean the restaurant staff must work hard so that customers can relax. I can't emphasize this enough. E2 For today's lecture, I'd like you to take the perspective of a restaurant owner. Pretend that you're someone like me, who starts a small restaurant because you love cooking and you love bringing enjoyment to people through food. Will this be enough to guarantee your customers satisfaction and your restaurant success? The answer is no. With my first restaurant, I had a great time cooking, but I didn't understand the restaurant as a business, and I lost lots of customers and lots of money. Unfortunately, this isn't uncommon. Many small, independent restaurants don't succeed. In fact, only about one in five lasts more than five years. And this may surprise you: More than half of all restaurants are independent, according to the U.S. National Restaurant Association. We see chain restaurants like Applebee's and Denny's everywhere, but actually, about half of all restaurants are independently owned. E3 So what's the key to a restaurant's success? As I said at the outset, there are many factors. But let's consider one of the most essential factors in the dining experience: ambience. First a restaurant owner has to decide what kind of social experience to create for customers. A fun place? Upscale? Romantic, perhaps? Then the owner must decide how to create that feeling. The type of

furniture, the lighting, the decorations, the music, the table arrangements, and the clothes that the staff wear are components that work together to create an overall feeling: ambience. E4 Now, going back to our original two concepts, I'm going to illustrate how ambience and other factors contribute to customer satisfaction, and how contrast rules the restaurant business, using an example. Let's suppose there is a couple, Justin and Kate. It's Kate's birthday. Justin decides to take Kate to an upscale, expensive Italian restaurant called Dante's. Justin calls and makes a reservation for Saturday night at 8:00 P.M. He tells them it's her birthday. E5 Let's consider Justin and Kate's expectations for Saturday night. As far as the ambience goes, their expectations are Dante's will be quiet, with soft music, tablecloths, candles and flowers, gentle lighting, and, of course, a very polite waitstaff. As for general expectations, Justin and Kate are looking forward to a special, memorable dinner. They want to feel pampered. They'd like the restaurant staff to pay attention and respond to their needs, so that everything flows smoothly. There's another factor that makes customers feel satisfied. Of course, they expect delicious food. Dante's is known for its creative menu. E6 If Justin and Kate are our typical customers, with high expectations, how can a restaurant owner like Dante meet those expectations? First off, the restaurant owner and the staff must have a clear understanding of everything they need to do to make customers happy. They must also expect to work hard and be very well organized. This is another factor in the success of a restaurant. E7 So, how does everything get done? Many restaurants like Dante's have a brigade system. A brigade is a group of workers. One brigade is at the front of the house. Here "house" means restaurant, of course. They take care of the tables. The other brigade is at the back of the house—the cooks and the chefs. They take care of the kitchen. A successful restaurant—the owner and the staff—knows how to balance the flow between the front of the house—where the customers are—and the back of the house—the kitchen. E8 Now, let's discuss in detail what happens at Dante's to prepare for a typical Saturday night. For the front of the house, the staff make sure the tables are ready; that everything is clean and in order: the flowers, the candles, the music, the lighting, the menus— everything that contributes to the ambience. For the back of the house, the staff focus on the food itself. E9 Now, back to Justin and Kate. They arrive at Dante's at 8:00 P.M., they're greeted, and they're led to a beautiful table in a quiet corner. They enjoy a long, leisurely dinner. At 10:00 P.M., they walk happily toward the door, feeling very content with the whole experience. E10 What were the two main reasons? Dante's understood what it needed to do both in the front of the house and the back of the house—from the ambience to the food—to meet their expectations. Plus, the restaurant staff worked hard so that Justin and Kate could do the opposite: relax. Success is built on understanding this contrast, remember. So keep these two concepts in mind as you consider your future as a restaurant owner.

Coaching Tips

[1] Note-taking: Noting subtopics The speaker first introduces the lecture's main topic: how to create a positive dining experience. Then he lists two subtopics he'll be discussing. What's a good way to note these subtopics? Here's one idea: [see video for note-taking example]. Notice that the subtopics are indented and numbered. By organizing your notes in this way, you can show how the ideas relate. It'll also help you understand your notes later.

Find audioscript for the other Coaching Tips at www.pearsonlongman.com/contemporarytopics.

Talk about the Topic *page 38*

Hannah: Yeah, so, I need a little help in understanding what, exactly, the "contrast" was in today's lecture. Can anyone explain it to me?

River: Sure, I'll try. He was trying to explain the difference between the relaxed experience of the guests, and the hard work of the staff.

Hannah: Ah-ha. But why is that important?

Manny: Well, I think he means that if you run a restaurant, you can measure your effort by how relaxed your guests are.

Mia: Did anyone notice that he put a lot of emphasis on ambience? I mean, that's fine. But personally, I'm more interested in the quality of the food.

Manny: Sorry to disagree, but I think that the ambience of a place can really affect your feelings about the food.

River: No way! You mean to say, if I have a burned steak I'm going to think it tastes great because there's beautiful music playing or there's beautiful flowers on the table?

Manny: No, of course not. What I'm saying is that a so-so steak will taste pretty good in an upscale place because the waitstaff is making you feel so relaxed.

Hannah: And the soft lighting is making you look good to your date.

Manny: Exactly! And meanwhile, your mouth doesn't notice or care that the food is just so-so.

Mia: OK. I can see that. Or, I guess if you're like Kate and Justin from the lecture, and you're in love, everything you experience together feels wonderful.

River: If that's the case, then I'm opening up a restaurant for couples in love only. That way, no one'll ever complain!

Take the Unit Test

1. What's the key to a successful restaurant?
2. What are the main concepts a restaurant owner must first understand? Choose *two* answers.
3. How does the speaker support his lecture?
4. What does the speaker mean by "success is built on contrast"?
5. Why does the speaker mention that many independent restaurants fail?
6. How many restaurants are independently owned?
7. What does the speaker think is one of the most essential factors in the dining experience?
8. The speaker describes Justin and Kate as "typical" customers. What does he mean by this?
9. How many brigades are in a restaurant?
10. How does the speaker feel about hard work and being well organized?

Extend the Topic *page 40*

Waiter: I've worked as a waiter for over twenty years. Some people say the customer is always right. Here's what I've figured out. Customers want to have a positive dining experience when they go out. But they have different expectations about what this means. So, I have to figure out very quickly what will make a customer satisfied. Some people want to be entertained. They want a waiter who is, well, a bit of an actor. With those customers, I have a good time. I have fun. I make jokes. Other customers just want good service and to be left alone. Others are out for a special occasion, say a wedding anniversary, and they want a lot of attention. I have to find the right balance with each table. It's a good feeling to know customers are satisfied. Of course, sometimes customers complain no matter what I do, but that goes with the job. For example, I once had . . .

Build Your Vocabulary *pages 33–34*

A. 1. atmosphere 2. give equal importance to
3. parts 4. difference 5. help to make happen
6. stressed 7. make certain 8. something as
different as possible 9. beginning 10. viewpoint
B. Interact with Vocabulary! 1. to 2. on 3. for
4. in 5. for 6. to 7. with 8. for 9. of 10. with

Focus Your Attention *page 35*

A. Main topic: waitstaff; subtopics: who makes up
the waitstaff, roles and responsibilities

Listen for Main Ideas *pages 36–37*

B. 1. b 2. c 3. c 4. b 5. c 6. a 7. b

Listen for Details *page 37*

B. 1. lasts 2. independent 3. social 4. furniture
5. rules 6. typical 7. menu 8. house 9. tables,
kitchen 10. flowed

Talk about the Topic *page 38*

A. *Suggested answers*: 1. River, Mia 2. Hannah,
Mia, Manny 3. Hannah, Mia, Manny **B.** 1. Asking
for clarification or confirmation 2. Paraphrasing
3. Paraphrasing 4. Asking for clarification or
confirmation 5. Agreeing

Review Your Notes *page 39*

I. **2 major customer service concepts:**
  1. many factors contribute to customer
    satisfaction
  2. successful experience is built on contrast

II. **Factors in creating ambience:**
  • type of social experience for customers
  • type of furniture, lighting, decorations,
    clothing, menu, tables, music, overall feeling

III. **How to meet customer expectations:**
  1. have a clear understanding of what needs to
    be done
  2. expect to work hard, be well organized

IV. **Brigade system**
  1. front of the house = waitstaff; takes care of
    tables
  2. back of the house = cooks/chefs; take care
    of kitchen

V. **Conclusions:**
  1. Kate and Justin very satisfied because
    Dante's knew what to do (many factors)
  2. Dante's staff worked very hard so that Kate
    and Justin could relax

Take the Unit Test

1. c 2. a and c 3. d 4. a 5. c 6. d 7. d 8. b 9. b
10. a

UNIT 4 TEST CULINARY ARTS: Owning a Successful Restaurant

 Listen to each question. Circle the letter of the correct answer.

1. a. preparing delicious food

b. providing nice ambience

c. knowing how to create a positive experience

d. using nice lighting and decorations

2. a. that many factors contribute to customers' satisfaction

b. that it's difficult to succeed as a restaurant owner

c. that a successful dining experience is built on contrast

d. that a skilled waitstaff is necessary

3. a. with facts about the restaurant industry

b. with examples from his own experience

c. with an imagined situation

d. all of the above

4. a. The staff works hard so customers can relax.

b. The food is upscale but the place is simple.

c. The food is simple and the place is fun.

d. The owner balances the work of the brigades.

5. a. to tell how chefs don't cook what people enjoy

b. to explain why the staff doesn't enjoy serving people

c. to show what happens if an owner doesn't understand the restaurant as a business

d. to argue that chain restaurants are too popular

6. a. about 1 out of five

b. about 1 out of fifteen

c. less than half

d. more than half

7. a. the food

b. the name

c. the location

d. the ambience

8. a. They are easy to please because they're in love.

b. They have high expectations because it's a special occasion.

c. They're dressed casually like everyone else at Dante's.

d. all of the above

9. a. one

b. two

c. three

d. four

10. a. They're essential for a successful restaurant.

b. They might be helpful in the back of the house.

c. They help create an exciting restaurant atmosphere.

d. They make owning a restaurant enjoyable.

EDUCATION
How We Each Learn Best

In this unit, students explore what we mean by *intelligence* and the variety of ways individuals learn best. The lecture focuses on the theory of multiple intelligences and the impact of that theory on teaching practices. Follow-up projects extend the topic to emotional intelligence and English sports idioms related to leadership, as well as an exploration of how different cultures value different intelligences.

Connect to the Topic   *page 42*   *~10 minutes*

Students read statements that represent various personality traits and learning styles. Students decide how well each statement describes them and then compare responses with a partner. For the final question—"What do (your responses) show about your personality or how you learn?"—consider providing the students with specific situations or examples to help them connect their scores to how they learn.

Build Your Vocabulary   *pages 43–44*   *~15 minutes*

Students study these words and phrases related to education and multiple intelligences:

accurately	impact on	(the) notion (that)
assess	(keep) in mind	options
aware (of)	interpreted to mean	sensitive to
brings up	kinesthetic	stands for
demonstrated	(intelligence)	think of
going over	logic	value
good at	mental	(a) variety of

For the Interact with Vocabulary! activity, you may want to encourage students to notice the boldfaced word in each sentence. When paired with the correct particle, these words form collocations, which are valuable in building students' vocabulary and fluency.

Focus Your Attention   *page 45*   *~10 minutes*

Students learn phrases that a speaker may use to tell how many ideas will be covered. They also learn how to organize their notes based on these kinds of phrases:

*There are **five steps** in the process . . .*
*I'm going to present **two techniques** . . .*
*I'm going to cover **three types** of learning styles . . .*

Listen to the Lecture   *pages 46–47*   *~30 minutes*

Prior to listening to the unit lecture, students write their ideas about what *multiple intelligences* means (Before You Listen). They then listen to the lecture and answer true/false questions (Listen for Main Ideas) and sentence completion questions (Listen for Details). *Lecture video time: 6 min. 37 sec.*   *Number of episodes: 10*

Talk about the Topic *page 48*

~20 minutes

Four students—Qiang, Yhinny, Michael, and May—discuss the lecture. Part A focuses on matching these students with ideas from the discussion. In Part B, your students work on identifying these discussion strategies:

- Expressing an opinion: "I don't think education is for developing those talents. . . . "
- Offering a fact or example: "OK. So, for example, this guy Anthony in my history class . . . "
- Asking for clarification or confirmation: "What do you mean?"

For Part C, students are encouraged to use the discussion strategies they've learned. They may use phrases from the student discussion and/or the Discussion Strategy box, or they may come up with their own. As an option for the third topic, students could demonstrate their approaches to the class.
Student discussion video time: 1 min. 52 sec.

Review Your Notes *page 49*

~15 minutes

Students focus on reconstructing their notes, paying attention to definitions, key ideas, and effects relating to multiple intelligences.

> **BONUS ACTIVITY**
>
> Have pairs of students choose a short lesson (such as categorizing trees) and decide how to teach it. They present their lesson to another pair, then that pair identifies the intelligences being utilized.

Take the Unit Test *Teacher's Pack page 31*

~15 minutes

You may want to play the lecture again just before giving the test. Students answer standard test questions about the content of the lecture. Specifically, the test covers the following: definition of the term *multiple intelligences*, examples of types of intelligences, applications of the theory in the classroom, and testing and assessment.

Extend the Topic *pages 50–51*

~30 minutes

- Listening and Discussion: Students listen to a clip about a person's unlikely path to success. Then they discuss what they heard.
- Reading and Discussion: Student read about emotional intelligence and learn sports idioms related to leadership and failure. They discuss whether emotional intelligence should be a factor in hiring by companies.
- Research and Presentation: Students explore the idea that different cultures value different intelligences. They are asked to consider the values within their own cultures, conduct research on another culture, and then make comparisons.

Focus Your Attention:
Try It Out! *page 45*

Speaker: We all know that we want any class that we teach to be successful. We want our students to learn. That's our goal as teachers, right? So, today, I'll present three teaching tips that are valuable in any classroom. The first tip is this: Engage your students. Make the class lively. Get students involved by asking questions, or by having them do something. The second tip: Make sure your students know what's expected of them. Even if you have to write it on the board, make sure they understand what you want them to do. And the third tip: Can anyone guess? . . .

Listen for Main Ideas and Listen
for Details *pages 46–47*

Education lecturer: E1 Today I'm going to talk about one theory in education that has had a big impact on the classroom. It's the theory of multiple intelligences. "Multiple" means "many." Intelligence is difficult to define. During today's class, as we discuss the theory of multiple intelligences, I'm going to use the term "intelligence" to mean "strength"—"a strong ability." This is a broader way of thinking about intelligence than usual. So first I'm going to go over the theory. Then, I plan to present how the theory has affected what some teachers now do in the classroom. **E2** Before I do that, I want to say a few words about how intelligence is often determined. As we all know, written IQ tests are still the main tool used to measure intelligence. "IQ," by the way, stands for "intelligence quotient"—"quotient" means "number." A high score on an IQ test, say 130, is interpreted to mean a person is very intelligent; a score of 100 is average. **E3** However, many factors can affect someone's score, including cultural background, education—or even the fact that they aren't good at taking tests. For these reasons, some people say traditional IQ tests don't accurately measure intelligence. Another reason to question IQ tests is the theory of multiple intelligences. Harvard University's Dr. Howard Gardner and others have explored the notion that we each have many types of intelligence. What makes us different from one another is which intelligences are stronger. **E4** Now I'm going to present nine intelligences they have identified. Keep in mind that they say we each have all of these intelligences. The first is verbal intelligence. People with strong verbal intelligence can speak and write well. This type of intelligence is valued in most schools and on written tests. The second is mathematical intelligence—the ability to work well with numbers and diagrams; think of someone who uses logic to solve problems and make decisions. The third is musical intelligence. People with strong musical intelligence, they feel sound; they feel music. They connect to sounds around them. **E5** Are you with me so far? OK. The fourth is artistic intelligence. People with strong artistic intelligence are sensitive to color, light, and shapes. They're good at drawing, painting, fashion, lots of creative things. The fifth kind of intelligence is spatial. We use spatial intelligence to create mental images to remember information. Think of someone who understands charts and maps easily; who has a good sense of direction, and doesn't get lost on mountain hikes. The sixth is kinesthetic or body intelligence; it's related to moving, to learning and remembering information by doing. The seventh is interpersonal intelligence; that's *inter*. Means "between" people. It's knowing how to work well with others in social situations, like work or school. **E6** The eighth is intrapersonal intelligence. "Intra" means "within one's self." It's about being uniquely aware of our own emotions and needs. For example, my brother John doesn't like crowds. He doesn't go to clubs or to the mall. He's happier alone or in a smaller group. The ninth kind of intelligence is nature intelligence—understanding one's connection with nature and the environment. Remember, the theory says we each have all of these intelligences. We just vary as to which intelligences are stronger. Think of your friends and what each is good at. **E7** So now I want to shift our discussion to the impact of the theory of multiple intelligences on teaching. If teachers accept the theory, how does this affect what they do in the classroom? There are two effects: One is on how they teach, the other is how they test their students. To teach, they need to use a variety of teaching techniques in order to reach the most students. What works best for one student might not work best for another. To test or assess what students understand, teachers need to give students options besides taking a written test. **E8** Let's use an example. As I give the example, I want you to write down the intelligences you can identify. OK? So, a teacher, Mrs. Sanchez, wants to teach her students about trees. Here's what she does: First, she talks about types of trees. She also draws a diagram on the board. Then they go outside, walk around, look at and touch trees near their school. Back in the classroom, she asks them to draw pictures of trees. Finally, she teaches them a song about trees. Did you get which intelligences she worked with when they went outside? How about when she had them draw pictures? **E9** All right. Now, she needs to test—or assess—what the students know. She gives them choices. For example, they can write about trees, draw a picture, make a chart, or create a song. Anything is acceptable as long as it contains the tree material she taught them. This is a key point. I realize you might think drawing a picture or creating a song isn't a "real" test. But, if we have multiple intelligences, what's the logical conclusion? Isn't it that students will benefit from using a variety of ways to demonstrate what they understood? A written test may not be the best way to assess every student. **E10** This brings up the whole issue of standardized tests, and whether they discriminate against students who don't have strong verbal and mathematical intelligences. For next time, think about this with regard to what you've heard today.

Coaching Tips

[1] Note-taking: Listing items The speaker tells you that she's about to present nine kinds of intelligences. Take a look at your notebook. Can you picture how you might note such a list? One idea is to pre-number your paper, in two columns, like this: [see video for note-taking example]. Be sure to leave room for the details!

Find audioscript for the other Coaching Tips at www.pearsonlongman.com/contemporarytopics.

Talk about the Topic *page 48*

Michael: Man, you know, this multiple intelligences theory is really interesting. Like, I know a lot of people who'd benefit from this theory.

May: What do you mean?

Michael: Well, I mean, I know a lot of people who are smart, but they're smart in different ways. I mean they're smart in ways that traditional IQ tests can't see.

Yhinny: I don't know, can you give me an example?

Michael: OK. So for example, this guy Anthony in my history class, he's failing the course and on test day, he's a mess—I mean he can't remember a single fact or a single date.

Qiang: But he's intelligent in some other way, you think?

Michael: Well, definitely! I mean, he's a sculptor, and he makes really beautiful pieces.

May: A sculptor? Like, he makes statues?

Michael: Yeah.

May: But is that really intelligence? Because it just sounds like talent.

Qiang: Actually, that's what I was going to say. You know, we can all think of talented athletes, singers—but are they really "intelligent"?

Michael: Well, I tend to argue, yes. I mean, what good is a high IQ, or high verbal or mathematical

ability? I mean, it doesn't necessarily mean that you're good at anything. It just means that you did well on an IQ test.

Yhinny: I'm with you. The multiple intelligences theory is more useful than an IQ test. It recognizes where a person is strong.

Michael: Right.

May: Or, talented, like I said. I don't think education is for developing those talents. It's for developing intelligence in those traditional areas. I'm sorry, that's just how I see it.

Michael: I mean, for me, I'd rather have a professor who sees me for my "multiple intelligences"—and not just how I do on written tests.

Qiang: Well, so have any of you taken one of those IQ tests?

Michael: I didn't do so well on mine. . . . I don't know—I'm amazing in other ways.

Take the Unit Test

1. What's another way to say "multiple intelligences"?
2. Which *doesn't* the speaker talk about?
3. Why don't some people like intelligence tests?
4. Which is true of the theory of multiple intelligences?
5. What does the speaker believe about all students?
6. What are two characteristics of someone with verbal intelligence?
7. Someone who uses logic to solve problems is using which intelligence?
8. Alex is a great leader and works well with others. Which intelligence does this show?
9. What is the speaker's attitude toward allowing students to write poems or songs?
10. How do you think the lecturer probably feels about standardized tests?

Extend the Topic *page 50*

Speaker: So now I want to ask: Does everyone remember that classmate who was obviously really intelligent? But somehow just couldn't get it together, academically? Well, there was this kid in my class—we called him Zack. In school, Zack got terrible grades. Reading and writing were especially hard for him. But we all knew he was smart—in his own way. When Zack was about fifteen, he helped his dad design a solar-chargeable battery. And it sold millions. He was totally brilliant with electronics. Brilliant. He understood things by *doing*, not by *reading*. Today, he's the owner of SunPower Systems and author of *Success My Way*. Please welcome, our guest speaker, Mr. Jeffrey Zackariason . . .

Build Your Vocabulary *pages 43–44*

B. 1. e 2. b 3. j 4. i 5. d 6. h 7. f 8. g 9. a 10. c
C. Interact with Vocabulary! 1. going 2. on 3. in
4. stands 5. at 6. of 7. mean 8. variety 9. sensitive
10. brings

Focus Your Attention *page 45*

A. Numbers and phrases: three teaching tips; The
first tip; The second tip; And the third tip . . . (not
mentioned)

Listen for Main Ideas *page 46*

B. 1. F (are not always) 2. T 3. F (the same
intelligences, but vary in strengths) 4. F (doesn't
emphasize any one intelligence) 5. T 6. F (not
necessarily the best way)

Listen for Details *page 47*

B. 1. having a strong ability in an area 2. 100
3. cultural background 4. mathematical
5. musical/verbal 6. reading a map 7. interpersonal
8. oneself 9. kinesthetic 10. about what she taught

Talk about the Topic *page 48*

A. 1. Qiang, May 2. Yhinny, Michael 3. Yhinny,
Michael **B.** 1. Asking for clarification or
confirmation 2. Asking for clarification or
confirmation 3. Offering a fact or example
4. Asking for clarification or confirmation
5. Expressing an opinion

Review Your Notes *page 49*

Def. of multiple intelligences: strengths/strong
abilities; **Traditional way to measure intelligence:**
IQ test; **Reasons some people don't like:** many
factors can influence a score, e.g., ability to take test,
cultural background, fact that it's a written test;
9 intelligences: 1. verbal: speak & write well;
2. mathematical: good with numbers, logic;
3. musical: feel sound, connect to it; 4. artistic:
sensitive to light, color, shapes; 5. spatial: creates
mental images to remember things, good with
charts, maps, direction; 6. kinesthetic (body): learn
by moving and doing; 7. interpersonal: work well
with others, strong social skills in groups;
8. intrapersonal: aware of one's needs, strong sense
of self; 9. nature: understanding one's connection
with nature; **2 impacts of multiple intelligences
theory in classroom:** 1. ways of teaching, 2. ways of
assessing; **Issue with standardized tests:**
discriminate against students who don't have strong
verbal skills, don't provide opportunity for students
to be assessed in a variety of ways

Take the Unit Test

1. c 2. d 3. b 4. d 5. a 6. b 7. c 8. a 9. d 10. b

 **EDUCATION: How We Each Learn Best**

 Listen to each question. Circle the letter of the correct answer.

1. a. multiple feelings

   b. multiple approaches

   c. multiple strengths

   d. multiple ideas

2. a. the theory of multiple intelligences

   b. nine kinds of multiple intelligences

   c. how the multiple intelligences theory affects a classroom

   d. why some people oppose the theory of multiple intelligences

3. a. because the average score is 100

   b. because they don't accurately measure all strengths

   c. because an above-average score is 130

   d. because they're often very long

4. a. Everyone has the same strengths.

   b. Everyone has all nine intelligences.

   c. Everyone has some intelligences that are stronger than others.

   d. both b and c

5. a. They need to be allowed to demonstrate their understanding in different ways.

   b. They have high IQs.

   c. They have strong verbal intelligence.

   d. They would benefit from a tree-drawing exercise.

6. a. has a good sense of direction and can identify shapes

   b. communicates well in words and uses language skillfully

   c. has a strong connection to nature and one's place in it

   d. has an ability to analyze visual images and charts

7. a. artistic

   b. kinesthetic

   c. mathematical

   d. spatial

8. a. interpersonal

   b. intrapersonal

   c. artistic

   d. kinesthetic

9. a. It's unfair to all of the students.

   b. It's less accurate than giving a written test.

   c. It makes it difficult to really assess students.

   d. It's reasonable, based on the multiple intelligences theory.

10. a. She finds them useful.

   b. She thinks they don't measure all types of intelligences.

   c. She believes they benefit most students.

   d. She thinks they discriminate against all students.

6 HISTORY
The Silk Road

TEACHING TIPS

UNIT OVERVIEW

In this unit, students learn about the Silk Road and consider factors and risks in the development of trade routes. The lecture focuses on Rome and China as the Silk Road developed. Follow-up projects extend the topic to global travel and business risks, the cultural impact of the Silk Road—for example, the spread of Buddhism—and the cultural impact of globalization.

Connect to the Topic *page 52*   *~10 minutes*

Students work with a map of the Silk Road, following the generally indicated routes and in place names. To further familiarize them with the geographical features of the Silk Road and the physical challenges that traders faced, consider providing students with an atlas or other detailed map.

Build Your Vocabulary *pages 53–54*   *~15 minutes*

Students study these words and phrases related to history and the Silk Road:

alternate (route)	dynasty	network (of
both . . . and . . .	estimates of	routes)
conflict (with)	for years	passed through
contact with	in particular	peak (period)
decade	in power	prosperous
decline	led to	recruit
defend against	length of	respectively

Focus Your Attention *page 55*   *~10 minutes*

Students learn to focus on dates, numbers, and chronologies, and to organize that information in tandem with the key ideas they hear. A chart is shown as an example, including the following:

Date	Key phrase	Details
206 BCE–220 CE	Han Dynasty	Silk Road developed

Listen to the Lecture *pages 56–57*   *~30 minutes*

Prior to listening to the unit lecture, students consider why the route was called "the Silk Road" (Before You Listen). Students then listen to the lecture and answer multiple-choice questions (Listen for Main Ideas) and true/false questions (Listen for Details).
Lecture video time: 6 min. 22 sec.   *Number of episodes: 12*

> **NOTE**
>
> Remember that with the DVD, you can play the lecture in different modes: video, video with subtitles, video with Coaching Tips, video with Presentation Points, video with Coaching Tips and subtitles, and video with Coaching Tips and Presentation Points. (We do not recommend playing the video with both the Presentation Points and subtitles on.) You can also play the lecture as audio only, using the CD.

Talk about the Topic *page 58*

~20 minutes

Four students—Ayman, Molly, Rob, and Alana—discuss the lecture. Part A focuses on matching these students with comments from the discussion. In Part B, your students work on identifying these discussion strategies:

- Asking for opinions or ideas: "So, do you guys think . . . "
- Offering a fact or example: "Kind of like businesspeople today . . . "
- Asking for clarification or confirmation: "Essentially, it was about trade, right?"

For Part C, students are encouraged to use the discussion strategies they've learned. They may use phrases from the student discussion, or they may come up with their own. As an extension of the third topic, ask students to consider parallels between the Silk Road and its trade centers, and global trade today.
Student discussion video time: 1 min. 37 sec.

Review Your Notes *page 59*

~15 minutes

Students focus on reconstructing their notes, paying attention to key dates and events. They should have enough details in their notes to go beyond the basic timeline.

> **BONUS ACTIVITY**
>
> You can supplement this activity by asking students to recreate a map of the Silk Road, including the routes and geographic features, and summarize why the Silk Road was so challenging to travel on.

Take the Unit Test *Teacher's Pack page 37*

~15 minutes

You may want to play the lecture again just before giving the test. Students answer standard test questions about the content of the lecture. Specifically, the test covers the following: reasons the Silk Road developed, Roman and Chinese history during that time, and reasons the Silk Road died out.

Extend the Topic *pages 60–61*

~15 minutes

- Listening and Discussion: Students listen to and discuss an extract from a TV travel show in which the guide describes the food at her next stop along the Silk Road.
- Reading and Discussion: Students read about the spread of Buddhism and the folktales of the Effendi Nasreddin, a Muslim folk hero. Then they discuss the cultural impact of globalization.
- Research and Presentation: Students conduct research on their choice of topics related to the Silk Road and prepare a short presentation.

Focus Your Attention:
Try It Out! *page 55*

Speaker: Good morning. In today's lecture, I'm going to present a little background leading up to the Silk Road, starting in the year 330 BCE. By the way, B-C-E stands for "before the common era." OK, so, in 330 BCE, Alexander the Great conquered a large area, the area that is roughly Iran, Syria, and Iraq today. There were some trade routes already there. But he wanted to develop more, and he did so. But not for long. Because in 325 BCE, the Romans attacked Alexander the Great, and won. So, it was in 325 BCE that the Romans took control of that region. Like Alexander, they, too, wanted to develop more trade routes. Why? In order to get luxury goods such as silk, spices, and gold. And by about 100 BCE, trading with China had begun, so the Romans were getting what they wanted . . .

Listen for Main Ideas and Listen for Details *pages 56–57*

History lecturer: E1 Today we're going to continue with a discussion of the Silk Road, one of the most historically important trade routes in the world. Now, as you know, the Silk Road was a major trade route between Europe and western China for about 1,500 years. It was used from about 100 BCE until about 1400 CE. There had been some trade across Central Asia before that, but it wasn't until about 100 BCE that trade between Europe and China increased significantly. E2 So, we're going to look at how the Silk Road developed. First, I want to mention three dynasties in China that were in power at significant points in the Silk Road's history. "Dynasty" here means "a group of rulers or a family with political control." First, the Han Dynasty. They ruled from 206 BCE to 220 CE, approximately when the Silk Road started. Second is the Tang Dynasty, in power from 618 to 907—the peak period of the Silk Road. And third, the Ming Dynasty. In 1368 they took control and soon thereafter the use of the Silk Road basically ended. Now this is just a quick overview, so I'll go into more detail about these three groups later. E3 Now most people say "the Silk Road," but it wasn't only one route. It was a network of routes between China and the Mediterranean Sea. The routes from China all started in Xi'an. That's spelled "X-i-apostrophe-a-n." I actually lived in Xi'an a few years back when I was working in China. And from Xi'an I traveled way out into western China just to get a sense of what the Silk Road was really like. It wasn't an easy

place to travel, but traders did it for many years. Now, going forward, you should know that Xi'an was actually called Chang'an during the time of the Silk Road. E4 So, from Chang'an, the route went west until traders reached the Taklamakan Desert. To avoid it, some routes went south through Dunhuang, and some went north through the Gobi Desert and over into Central Asia. The routes all reconnected further west, though, and eventually they led to some big trade centers in Europe in Rome and what is now called Istanbul in Turkey. There are different estimates about how long the Silk Road was altogether. We're going to go with about 5,000 miles—or 8,000 kilometers. E5 So, what do you think was the main reason the Silk Road developed? Well, the short answer is that people in Europe wanted goods from China, and people in China wanted goods from Europe. I'll focus now on the west end of the route, in Europe. And then we'll go to the east end, in China. On the west end, at the Mediterranean Sea, were the Romans. By about 100 BCE, the Romans had learned about luxury goods from China—silk in particular, which was very popular in Rome then. So, the Romans started building roads to the east so they could get luxury goods from China. Meanwhile, from the east end in China, the Han Dynasty was in power. E6 We have to review a little history at this point: The Han Dynasty ruled, ruled China from 206 BCE to 220 CE, as I mentioned. And Chang'an was the capital. But because China was so big, it was very difficult to defend, especially against the Mongol invaders from the north. So in 138 BCE, Emperor Wudi, that's W-u-d-i, sent a group out to western China to recruit fighters for the conflict with the Mongol invaders. The group's leader was captured. And when he returned a decade later, he told the emperor about a type of big, strong horse in western China. The Han Dynasty decided to make a big push west to get these horses in order to make the Han army stronger. E7 So, you see, in about 100 BCE, the Romans and the Chinese were pushing east and west, respectively, and thus the Silk Road developed. E8 According to historical records, the Romans didn't go all the way to China, and the Chinese traders didn't go all the way to Europe. Instead, many of the traders were from Central Asia. The traders mostly went short distances in caravans, and bought and sold goods along the way. Europe wanted silk, spices, and furs, and other goods from China. China wanted horses, initially. But later it wanted goods from Europe like gold and glass. E9 And traders exchanged both goods and information. For example, there were trade secrets, like where to get the best silk and where the best routes were. The Silk Road was very difficult to travel, and traders tried alternate routes mainly to avoid two things: bad weather and bad people. There were many robbers who tried to steal the traders' silk and other goods. Traders also wanted to avoid towns that forced them to pay a fee when passing through. **E10** The peak period for the Silk Road was in the 600s during the Tang Dynasty. Chang'an was very big and very prosperous then. About 2 million people lived there, including 8,000 foreigners from many places including what is today Iran, Turkey, Japan, and Korea. By the early 900s, the Tang Dynasty lost power, and trade on the Silk Road declined sharply because there was fighting and it became much too dangerous for the traders. **E11** By about 1400, trade on the Silk Road basically stopped. There were two main reasons: One, in 1368, the Ming Dynasty took control, and they didn't want any contact with foreigners. And two, European traders began to prefer ships, which were faster and safer than the Silk Road. **E12** So, to wrap up: The Silk Road developed because people in one part of the world wanted something from another part of the world. In recent years, people have talked about globalization as creating new Silk Roads. We'll take up this idea next time, OK?

Coaching Tips

[1] **Note-taking: Using timelines** History lectures like this one often have a lot of important dates and numbers. You've heard some already, right? And there's more to come! A timeline is another great way to track dates. Here's an example of how you may have noted the information you've heard so far: [see video for note-taking example].

Find audioscript for the other Coaching Tips at www.pearsonlongman.com/contemporarytopics.

Talk about the Topic *page 58*

Molly: I'd heard of the Silk Road before, but I had no idea it was so complicated! I mean, my notes look like a page from a math book!

Rob: Right.

Alana: Oh, mine, too. So, can we go over some of these dates? I mean, I think I got the general idea—that China wanted goods from Europe, and Europe wanted goods from China, and therefore the Silk Road was developed. Right?

Rob: Right. I have that the route was used from about 100 BCE to 1400 CE.

Molly: So it was in use for about 1,500 years, and it was about 5,000 miles long altogether, right?

Alana: Oh yeah, yeah. So, do you guys think the Silk Road is famous because of the goods traded? Or is it historic because of the cultural exchange that happened?

Rob: The Romans wanted luxury items from China, right? Especially the silk.

Alana: Uh-huh.

Rob: So essentially it was about trade, right?

Molly: Well, yeah, I mean, that's factually correct. But I think something deeper was going on, you know? I mean—cultures were mixing.

Ayman: Oh yeah, like Central Asian traders. They had a very important job, like being a "middleman."

Alana: Yeah, exactly. Without them, the whole exchange of goods wouldn't have happened.

Rob: But it was probably a pretty dangerous job, too. I mean, if you think about it, they had to go out and communicate with people from different cultures with different languages, and had to exchange goods with them. I mean, that must have been pretty risky.

Alana: Kind of like businesspeople today—trying to make money and survive.

Molly: Yeah, I guess not that much has changed in the past two thousand years!

Take the Unit Test

1. For how many years was the Silk Road a major trade route?
2. When did trade between Rome and China increase significantly?
3. Why does the speaker say the term "*the* Silk Road" is actually incorrect?
4. During the time of the Silk Road, what was Xi'an known as?
5. What was the Han Dynasty's big problem?
6. Why did Emperor Wudi want horses from western China?
7. Why were most of the Silk Road traders from Central Asia?
8. Why did trade drop off when the Tang Dynasty lost power?
9. The Ming Dynasty closed China to foreigners. What was the other main reason trade on the Silk Road stopped?
10. What aspect of the Silk Road did the lecturer *not* mention?

Extend the Topic *page 60*

Marta: Today's stop along the Silk Road finds us in the busy city of Urumqi, located in northwestern China. Because of its proximity to countries like Mongolia, Kazakhstan, and Pakistan, Urumqi has long been considered the gateway to Central Asia. In the days of the Silk Road, Urumqi's location was perfect for traders. And today? It's perfect for adventure travelers like myself who love trying delicious, exotic foods. So with the help of local guide Hom Wang, we're going to plan a picnic to nearby Heavenly Lake.

Hom: What a great idea, Marta. Let's first pick up some nan chao rou, a popular dish here made with flatbread, lamb, and red pepper.

Marta: Yum! What else?

Hom: Well, our side dish is going to be daal from a little Pakistani shop I love. It's made with tomatoes, garlic, butter, and lentil beans. You can eat it with bread or crackers. And, for dessert, we'll stop by the market and buy some delicious watermelon.

Marta: Sounds fantastic! And to drink? Let me guess—tea!

Hom: You said it. With milk and salt, of course—the Kazakh way!

Marta: Sounds great. I can't wait! . . .

ANSWER KEY

Build Your Vocabulary *pages 53–54*

B. 1. recruit 2. network 3. prosperous 4. decline 5. decade 6. conflict 7. dynasties 8. respectively 9. peak 10. alternate **C. Interact with Vocabulary!** 1. in/for 2. to/in 3. of/of 4. from/in 5. against/from 6. through/in 7. both/and

Focus Your Attention *page 55*

A.

Date	Event	Details
330 BCE	Silk Road begins	
330 BCE	Alexander the Great conquers large area; wants to develop more routes	Area today is Iran, Syria and Iraq
325 BCE	Romans attack Alexander the Great/ win; also want more route for luxury goods	Luxury goods include silk, spices, gold
100 BCE	Romans trading w/China, getting the goods they want	

Listen for Main Ideas *page 56*

B. 1. b 2. b 3. c 4. a 5. c

Listen for Details *page 57*

B. 1. F (1,500 years) 2. F (100 BCE) 3. T 4. T 5. F (recruit soldiers for his army) 6. T 7. T 8. F (8,000 foreigners) 9. F (by the 900s) 10. F (by 1400)

Talk about the Topic *page 58*

A. 1. Molly 2. Alana 3. Rob **B.** 1. Asking for opinions or ideas 2. Asking for clarification or confirmation 3. Offering a fact or example 4. Offering a fact or example

Review Your Notes *page 59*

206–220 Han Dynasty: Silk Road begins in earnest; 600s–900s Tang Dynasty: peak period; 1368 Ming Dynasty: takes control; 1400 trade stops

Take the Unit Test

1. b 2. c 3. c 4. d 5. a 6. a 7. b 8. c 9. c 10. b

HISTORY: The Silk Road

Listen to each question. Circle the letter of the correct answer.

1. a. 600 years
   b. 1,500 years
   c. 1,000 years
   d. 2,000 years

2. a. 220 BCE
   b. 200 BCE
   c. 100 BCE
   d. 220 CE

3. a. because the route went north over the Gobi Desert
   b. because more than just silk was traded along the way
   c. because it was more than one road; it was a large network of routes
   d. because it led to big trade centers in Europe, not Asia

4. a. Rome
   b. Dunhuang
   c. Istanbul
   d. Chang'an

5. a. Mongol invaders from the north
   b. the Taklamakan Desert
   c. the Gobi Desert
   d. too many foreigners

6. a. to strengthen his army
   b. to increase trade with Central Asia
   c. to develop trade with Rome
   d. to make Chang'an prosperous

7. a. because the European traders didn't want to pay fees when passing through towns
   b. because traveling the entire route would be too far for European and Chinese traders
   c. because robbers would steal from the Asian traders
   d. because the weather was very bad on parts of most routes

8. a. because it was the peak period
   b. because traders wanted to avoid fees
   c. because it became too dangerous
   d. because many foreigners lived in Chang'an

9. a. There was no more silk.
   b. Traders wanted to avoid fees.
   c. Traders wanted to use ships.
   d. The Romans controlled the routes.

10. a. the goods traded
    b. the traders' housing
    c. the ruling Chinese dynasties
    d. the geography

TEACHING TIPS

UNIT OVERVIEW

In this unit, students will explore one aspect of the business world: team building. The lecture focuses on issues related to building an effective team and the steps that a manager takes. Follow-up projects extend the topic to conflict resolution, cultural differences about time, and research on a company culture.

Connect to the Topic *page 62*   *~10 minutes*

As they consider their own values, students read a list of statements reflecting values, and check those they agree with. They then compare responses with a partner.

Build Your Vocabulary *pages 63–64*   *~15 minutes*

Students study these words and phrases related to business and team building:

accomplish	interference with	responsible for
challenge	lead to	sufficient (for)
chemistry between	on time	suited for
(an) effective (manager)	(a good) practice	summary
enhance	project	vital
fit in	pull together	a waste of time
got started on	resolve (conflicts)	zero in on
in summary		

After the Interact with Vocabulary! activity, you may want to have students practice using the boldfaced words with their partners. Knowing collocations can help students expand their vocabularies and increase their fluency.

Focus Your Attention *page 65*   *~10 minutes*

Students focus on taking notes more quickly by using the following symbols and abbreviations:

e.g. or ex. – for example	**#** – amount OR number of
etc. – additional persons or things	**=** – is OR equals
i.e. – in other words	**≠** – isn't OR doesn't equal
& – and	**x** – number of times (**2x**)
@ – at	**→** – causes OR results in
↑ – increase	**?** – question
↓ – decrease	

Listen to the Lecture *pages 66–67*   *~30 minutes*

Prior to listening to the unit lecture on team building in business, students write down what they consider the qualities of a good manager (Before You Listen). Students listen to the lecture and answer multiple-choice questions (Listen for Main Ideas) and true/false questions (Listen for Details).

Lecture video time: 6 min. 51 sec.   *Number of episodes: 8*

Talk about the Topic *page 68*   *~20 minutes*

Four students—River, Mia, Manny, and Hannah—discuss the lecture. Part A focuses on matching these students with ideas from the discussion. Note that here students are checking who *disagrees* with the statement. In Part B, your students work on identifying three discussion strategies:

- Disagreeing: "Really? That seems like the fun part to me."
- Keeping the discussion on topic: "Anyway, back to the steps."
- Trying to reach a consensus: "What do you say we take a break and refill—to build our team?"

For Part C, students are encouraged to use the discussion strategies they've learned. They may use phrases from the student discussion and/or the Discussion Strategy box, or they may come up with their own.

> **NOTE**
>
> Part C is a good opportunity for vocabulary development. As students discuss group chemistry and trust, try compiling their ideas on the board so that they can learn new words and phrases from each other.

Student discussion video time: 1 min. 33 sec.

Review Your Notes *page 69*   *~15 minutes*

Students focus on using their notes to paraphrase the main ideas of the lecture.

> **BONUS ACTIVITY**
>
> Have students use what they learned in the lecture to brainstorm ways that team building might be approached differently in a virtual team—that is, a team in which people are not in the same building to hold face-to-face meetings and therefore can't engage in traditional social activities.

Take the Unit Test *Teacher's Pack page 43*   *~15 minutes*

You may want to play the lecture again just before giving the test. Students answer standard test questions about the content of the lecture. Specifically, the test covers the following: teams versus groups,   steps a manager follows to form a team, building trust, and cultural considerations regarding social activities.

Extend the Topic *pages 70–71*   *~30 minutes*

- Listening and Discussion: Students listen to and discuss a telephone conversation between a new hire and a career hotline counselor.
- Reading and Discussion: Students read about several English expressions related to time. Then they consider what it means to be on time or late in their home cultures.
- Research and Presentation: Students research the culture of a company they are interested in and present their findings to the class.

Focus Your Attention:
Try It Out! *page 65*

Speaker: Well, we know that more and more, work is being done in teams. And, it's common to work on teams with people from different countries. This is true whether your office is in, for example, New York, or Paris, or Tokyo. So, what does it take to succeed on a global business team? I'm going to give you some questions that I want you to think about. Number one: In business there's been a big increase in the number of global teams. Do you have the teamwork skills needed? Two: Are you a risk taker? In other words, are you open to new experiences? Three: Are you curious about new ideas? For example, are you interested in learning why people from different cultural backgrounds think the way they do? . . .

Listen for Main Ideas and Listen for Details *pages 66–67*

Business lecturer: **E1** You'll remember in the last class we got started on styles of management. That's a very broad topic, so today I want to zero in on team building. It's an essential part of good management practices, so it's important that we spend some time on this. **E2** To begin: What's the difference between a team and a group? Think of a group as just some people together; they may know each other, they may not. How is a team different? Here are three characteristics: One: The people share a common goal. Two: They depend on each other to reach that goal. Three: Together they are responsible for what the team accomplishes. Anyone who's been on a sports team knows that a new team can feel more like a group of strangers. You don't know each other, you don't know how to work together. A skillful coach, though, can make that group into a strong team. Team building in business is similar. A skillful manager knows what to do. **E3** Let's use an example. There's a company called RZDesign, an advertising company. RZDesign has just won a big contract to do an ad campaign for a cosmetics company. The work needs to be completed within six months. This is the team's common goal. Tina is the project manager. She's hired some new employees. She needs to pull together a strong team of both old and new employees as quickly as possible. They have to do their best work to get the campaign done on time. **E4** Let's look at the specific steps that Tina takes to build her team. Step 1: She goes over all the work that needs to be done to complete the campaign. Step 2: She makes an assessment of the skills of the employees, both old and new. She recognizes that they have different abilities and strengths. She asks herself: Who is best suited for each task on the campaign? Step 3: She holds meetings with the whole team. They discuss the project. She assigns roles and makes it clear what each person is responsible for. **E5** Step 4: Tina identifies one main challenge: building trust on the team quickly. She considers trust vital to the team's success. Trust develops as team members learn who they can rely on to do their part, who they can depend on. Trust takes time to develop and, remember, she has only six months to complete the campaign. Step 5: To help build trust, Tina addresses two areas. Number one: Communication within the team. Tina explains to team members how she wants them to communicate with each other. She, she specifies in which situations they should use e-mail, voicemail, video conferencing, IMing, and so on. The second area of trust building Tina addresses is the team "chemistry." By this I mean, how the personalities of the team fit together. A basic consideration here is, what is each person on the team like? Who's efficient? Fun-loving? Quiet? Talkative? An independent thinker? And how do they each approach work? If team members are very different, this can cause conflicts and make it difficult to build a team feeling. **E6** This takes us to Step 6: Tina decides to use face-to-face meetings to resolve conflicts as they arise. Some people feel that e-mail and voicemail are sufficient, but sometimes you need to have people talking in the same room. So Tina sends out an e-mail announcing that there'll be a team meeting every Wednesday at nine o'clock. She keeps the meetings short so that members don't see them as a waste of their time or an interference with their work. The meetings need to enhance the team effort. At these meetings, she gives team members an opportunity to discuss and resolve problems. **E7** So another way to build trust is for the members to get to know each other better, which leads us to Step 7. Tina plans two activities for the whole team: a team picnic and a dinner, so they can relax together, outside of work. Some of you may be asking yourselves: Is it important for Tina to plan these activities? If they have a big contract, isn't it better to spend their time getting their work done? It's really hard to say. It depends on who's on the team. In some South American or Asian countries, like Brazil or Japan, people do things to build the relationships first, with the idea that the work will be better if they do. If you're from these countries, then you know what I'm talking about. But in the U.S., for example, the idea is more: jump in, get the work going first, and then the relationships will build within the team as the work gets done. It brings us back to how to build trust. If there are team members from different cultural backgrounds, they may disagree about how important the "fun stuff" is. An effective manager needs to consider this. E8 So, in summary, I've said that building trust is vital to team building. And good communication is an important part of the trust-building step. In your study sessions, please review the steps Tina takes and discuss why they're important. That's all for today.

Coaching Tips

[1] Note-taking: Using abbreviations and symbols
Some speakers give information very quickly, or maybe just a lot of it at once. Using abbreviations is a great "short-cut" for taking down lots of information quickly. For example, when a speaker gives a new term and definition, you can use the equals sign after the term to show that the words that follow is the definition. Here's a sample of symbols and abbreviations you might find useful for this lecture. [See video for note-taking example.]
Find audioscript for the other Coaching Tips at www.pearsonlongman.com/contemporarytopics.

Talk about the Topic *page 68*

Mia: I suggest we just go around and cover the seven steps to team building, OK?

Hannah: Sure, I'll start. So, first, if you're the manager of a project, you need to assess what the work is—what the contract asks for. Right?

River: Yeah.

Manny: Yup.

Mia: Yeah.

Hannah: Then you look at your employees and see who's best suited for different jobs.

Manny: Right. Next, you meet with the whole team to explain the project and then assign roles.

River: Then there's the trust building part.

Manny: Oh yeah, the "chemistry" part. I found that really interesting—I've had some managers that were terrible at understanding this step!

Mia: And professors! I think we're lucky. Our study group has good chemistry, and even though some of us are a little more talkative than others—like myself! Anyway, back to the steps.

Hannah: So I have a question about the next step: Do you guys agree that a team really needs face-to-face meetings? I mean, who has time?

River: I can understand it—you know, for conflicts, at least. But it's that next step—those team-building activities? I don't have the patience for office picnics or team bowling night. I spend all day with these people! I don't want to spend my free time with them, too!

Hannah: Really? That seems like the fun part to me.

Manny: Me, too. Well, what do you say we take a break and refill—to build our team?

Mia: Sounds good!

Take the Unit Test

1. How does the lecturer organize the lecture?
2. In the lecture, which of the following is *not* mentioned as a characteristic of a team member?
3. How are effective managers and coaches alike?
4. What is team building an essential part of? Choose *two* answers.
5. In the lecturer's example, what does Tina identify as her main challenge?
6. What does Tina do to build team trust?
7. Which is probably true of a team with good chemistry?
8. What is the speaker's attitude toward face-to-face meetings?
9. Which statement best represents the speaker's opinion about social activities?
10. What does the speaker conclude is vital to team building?

Extend the Topic *page 70*

Sandy: Don't Quit Your Day Job Hotline. This is Sandy, how can I help?

Caller: Hi, uh, Sandy. Um, so, I'm calling about my new job . . .

Sandy: Yeah, how's that going?

Caller: Not good. I'm supposed to send my designs to this guy, Todd, to review. He's the production manager, so he has to go over my designs, approve them, right?

Sandy: Uh-huh.

Caller: And, well, he hasn't responded to my e-mails for over a week. So, now I'm behind schedule big time.

Sandy: Have you tried talking directly to Todd about this?

Caller: He hasn't been around. Plus, he's been with the company a long time. And I'm, you know, a new hire. I don't want to cause problems. I've got to do something, though. The schedule is tight.

Sandy: So, talk to your boss. Find out what's going on.

Caller: OK. I should do that. I'm so stressed out. It's clear I can't rely on this guy Todd to do his part right now. It's messing up the whole project. And, I don't want everyone to think it's my fault if we're late.

Sandy: Take this to your manager. This is part of his or her job—managing the team.

Caller: Yeah. I guess I'll bring it up at my weekly meeting with her.

Sandy: Good idea. Good luck, kiddo . . .

ANSWER KEY

Build Your Vocabulary *pages 63–64*
B. 1. e 2. b 3. d 4. a 5. c 6. f 7. g 8. i 9. l 10. h
11. j 12. k **C. Interact with Vocabulary!** 1. between
2. on 3. for 4. on 5. for 6. in 7. In 8. with 9. to
10. of

Focus Your Attention *page 65*
A. words/phrases noted as symbols or abbreviations:
e.g. or ex, #1, ↑ in # of, #2, i.e., #3, e.g. or ex.

Listen for Main Ideas *page 66*
B. 1. c 2. b 3. c 4. b 5. b

Listen for Details *page 67*
B. 1. T 2. F (some were just hired) 3. F (six
months) 4. F (go over the work to be done) 5. T
6. F (decides to use face-to-face meetings) 7. T 8. F
(so team members don't see them as a waste of time)
9. T 10. F (to plan social activities based on the
cultural backgrounds of team members)

Talk about the Topic *page 68*
A. 1. Manny 2. Mia 3. Hannah 4. River
B. 1. Trying to reach a consensus 2. Keeping the
discussion on topic 3. Disagreeing 4. Trying to
reach a consensus

Take the Unit Test
1. c 2. c 3. d 4. b and d 5. a 6. b 7. d 8. b 9. c
10. a

UNIT 7 TEST BUSINESS: Team Building

 Listen to each question. Circle the letter of the correct answer.

1. a. by describing the qualities of a good manager

   b. by comparing team-building techniques

   c. by describing team-building steps

   d. by comparing team members' cultural backgrounds

2. a. shares a goal with team members

   b. depends on other team members

   c. always wants to win

   d. is responsible for team accomplishments

3. a. They don't believe in cooperation.

   b. They want to control everyone.

   c. They don't know how to work together.

   d. They can change a group into a team.

4. a. an employee's role

   b. a manager's job

   c. face-to-face meetings

   d. a team's success

5. a. building trust quickly

   b. talking to the employees

   c. assessing skills

   d. holding team meetings

6. a. assess the abilities of team members

   b. address communication and chemistry

   c. e-mail team members every day

   d. assign roles to members of the team

7. a. Its members prefer to work independently.

   b. Its members are very competitive.

   c. Its members don't get along very well.

   d. Its members enjoy working together on a project.

8. a. She considers them a waste of time.

   b. She sees the value of having people talk in person.

   c. She prefers e-mail.

   d. She thinks voicemail is just as good.

9. a. It's important to have a lot of them.

   b. Employees all seem to enjoy them.

   c. A manager needs to consider everyone's cultural background.

   d. A manager needs to start out with some.

10. a. building trust

   b. working late

   c. going to social activities

   d. working on the contract

TEACHING TIPS

UNIT OVERVIEW

In this unit, students explore the fundamental principles underlying all architecture by considering the work of architect Frank Gehry. The lecture focuses on Gehry's distinctive style. Follow-up projects extend the topic to types of unusual architecture and an exploration of jobs within the "green" economy, including "green" architecture.

Connect to the Topic *page 72* ~*10 minutes*

Students discuss features of the three buildings pictured, as well as their favorite buildings, in order to stimulate interest in building design and architecture. The words *architecture, design,* and *engineering* are introduced.

Build Your Vocabulary *pages 73–74* ~*15 minutes*

Students study these words and phrases related to architecture and Frank Gehry's work:

aesthetic consideration of	experimented with	principle
aesthetically pleasing to	foundation (of architecture)	principles of
aesthetics	innovation/innovative/	sculptor/sculpture
at the foundation of	innovator	(structurally) sound
distinct	inspirational	stress
distinguish from that of	intended use (of a building)	styles of
dynamic (style)	looks like	use of
emphasis on	met the objective	utilize

After the Interact with Vocabulary! activity, you may want to have students practice using the boldfaced words with their partners. Knowing collocations can help students expand their vocabularies and increase their fluency.

Focus Your Attention *page 75* ~*10 minutes*

Students learn phrases that lecturers use to emphasize or signal important ideas, as well as phrases used to check in to see if students are following the lecture. For example:

Signaling emphasis
To highlight what I've said so far . . .
I want to emphasize that . . .
I want to stress . . .
It's important to understand . . .

Checking in
Is everyone clear on this?
Is this clear?
Are there any questions?
Are you with me?

Listen to the Lecture *pages 76–77* ~*30 minutes*

Prior to listening to the unit lecture on architecture, students decide on the top three considerations an architect should have in mind when designing a building (Before You Listen). Then they listen to the lecture and answer multiple-choice questions (Listen for Main Ideas) and true/false questions (Listen for Details).
Lecture video time: 6 min. 37 sec. *Number of episodes: 13*

> **NOTE**
>
> Remember that with the DVD, you can play the lecture in different modes: video, video with subtitles, video with Coaching Tips, video with Presentation Points, video with Coaching Tips and subtitles, and video with Coaching Tips and Presentation Points. (We do not recommend playing the video with both the Presentation Points and subtitles on.) Note that while the DVD is compatible with most computer media players, for optimum viewing we suggest playing the DVD on a television using a DVD player. You can also play the lecture as audio only, using the CD.

Talk about the Topic   *page 78*   *~20 minutes*

Four students—Michael, Yhinny, May, and Qiang—discuss the lecture. Part A focuses on matching these students with ideas from the discussion. Note that here students are checking who *disagrees* with the statement. In Part B, your students work on identifying these discussion strategies:

- Asking for opinions or ideas: "OK, then what would you say about his engineering abilities . . . ?"
- Agreeing: "OK, sure, I can see that."
- Disagreeing: "What? I wouldn't say that."

For Part C, students are encouraged to use the discussion strategies they've learned. They may use phrases from the student discussion or they may come up with their own. To expand the second topic, ask students to address the broader question of the role of the artist in society— the balance between aesthetics and practical applications of one's skills.
Student discussion video time: 1 min. 42 sec.

Review Your Notes   *page 79*   *~15 minutes*

Students focus on reconstructing their notes, paying attention to ideas the speaker stressed.

> **BONUS ACTIVITY**
>
> Have students find additional examples of Gehry's buildings online, and discuss them based on the three features of Gehry's style and the three principles of Vitruvius.

Take the Unit Test   *Teacher's Pack page 49*   *~15 minutes*

You may want to play the lecture again before giving the test. Students answer standard test questions about the content of the lecture. Specifically, the test covers the following: the three principles of Vitruvius, Gehry's development as an architect, the three features of Gehry's style, and Gehry's reasons for his style.

Extend the Topic   *pages 80–81*   *~30 minutes*

- Listening and Discussion: Students listen to and discuss a TV show clip about unusual architecture.
- Reading and Discussion: Students read about and discuss "going green."
- Research and Presentation: Students choose a style of architecture to research and present on. Topics include mimetic architecture, which advertises the business it contains.

AUDIOSCRIPT

Focus Your Attention:
Try It Out! *page 75*

Speaker: OK, let's move on. Now I want to tell you the term we use to explain the reason a building is built. We say "the program" of a building to mean the reason for building it. For example, think about churches, mosques, and temples. The program for these is religion, right? What about theaters, sports stadiums, concert halls, and clubs? Places we go to have fun. The program for these is entertainment. Now, it's important to understand why we specify the program of a building. Often there are a lot of people involved in designing a building. So we want everyone to keep in mind what we're designing it for. Are you with me? Good. Now, before I go on, I want to highlight what I've said so far. *Program* is the term for the reason a building is built. Any questions?

Listen for Main Ideas and Listen for Details *pages 76–77*

Architecture lecturer: **E1** OK. Today we're going to talk about Frank Gehry, one of my favorite architects. If you've seen any of the buildings he's designed, like the Dancing House in Prague, you'll know why. It's a wonderful, colorful building near the river. Many tourists go to see it. But today, we'll consider Frank Gehry's work not as tourists, but as architects. **E2** It's understood that architecture is both the science and the art of designing buildings. We use science to make sure that the building is strong. And we use art because we want the building to be beautiful. In other words, we think about the aesthetics—or artistic value—of the building. **E3** Now here I want to mention Vitruvius, the Roman architect who lived in the first century BCE. He said that a building must have three fundamental characteristics: one, meet its intended use; two, be sound (which means strong); and three, be beautiful. He wrote these ideas 2,000 years ago, and they're still the foundation of architecture today. **E4** Let's go over these three characteristics in depth: First, a building must meet its intended use. Architects must think about the reason the building is being built as they design it. For example, the intended use for a school is a place to learn, right? Here architects must ask themselves: What type of design is best for both students and teachers? Second, a building must be structurally sound. What do I mean by this? I mean the design must follow these basic principles: Is it safe? Will it last a long time? Will it protect people from bad weather? Architects agree that a building must be able to do all of these things. **E5** Third, a building must be beautiful. Aesthetics is a harder principle to agree on. And, buildings last a long time if they're built properly. And so something built fifty years ago may not be considered beautiful now. Styles in architecture change, like with clothes or cars. All right, to highlight what I've said thus far: In addition to meeting the intended use, a building's design must also be structurally sound and aesthetically pleasing to people. Is everyone clear on this? **E6** Now, I'd like to shift to talking about Frank Gehry's work, and how he applied these three characteristics of architecture. Have any of you seen his buildings? Like the Walt Disney Concert Hall in Los Angeles? Or the Fish Dance restaurant in Kobe, Japan, that looks like a gigantic fish? I see a few hands, great. Then you'll know what I mean when I say his style is very distinct. He was an architectural pioneer who wasn't afraid to try new ideas. His designs are exciting and inspirational because they push us to explore the possibilities. **E7** Specifically, how can we describe his style? I can think of three words: resourceful, playful, and innovative. It's resourceful because of the building materials. It's playful because of the bright colors and fun designs—like his store in Venice, California, with giant binoculars at the entrance. And, it's innovative because he said good-bye to traditional architecture and experimented with new ideas. **E8** Now let's look at these three descriptions one at a time. Resourceful. In the 1970s, Gehry started utilizing simple building materials in his designs, like sheet metal and plywood. In fact, he's famous for using chain-link fence, the kind of fence you see around construction sites to keep people out. (I'm sure you've all seen it around a building being built.) Since he knew the fencing would always be there, he decided to use it in his designs. For example, he designed a mall in California with a huge wall—six stories high—covered in chain-link fence! (He went on to use other materials, of course, but started there.) **E9** Playful. His designs use bright, bold colors like yellow, orange, blue, and gold. Examples include the EMP Museum in Seattle and the DG Bank Building in Germany. **E10** And finally, innovative. Many of his buildings don't have straight walls. He uses irregular angles and shapes. A great example of this is the Vitra Design Museum in Germany. That's V-i-t-r-a. The building looks like it could fall down, to be honest. But of course it won't because Gehry designed it to be structurally sound. **E11** So how did Gehry develop his dynamic style? Up until the early 1970s, he did traditional architecture. However, he didn't feel it allowed him to be creative enough. He began experimenting with his design ideas by working on houses, including his own house in Santa Monica, California, which he worked on from 1977 to 1978. Many neighbors didn't like the design of his house, but Gehry did. E12 Now we ask, why did he develop this distinct style? He once said that he thinks like an artist. For him, a building is like a big sculpture or a big work of art. He pushes the limits of what is structurally possible from an engineering standpoint in order to create beautiful buildings. But I want to stress, he's also said that he always keeps in mind that a building is a sculpture that people interact with. If the building doesn't please them as a work of art and meet the intended use, he's failed in his objective. E13 In closing, I want to say that Frank Gehry is a noteworthy architect because his work challenges me and other architects to consider how to use simple materials while designing strong, beautiful, and purposeful structures. Now go build something.

Coaching Tips

[1] Critical Thinking: Identifying point of view
Why do you think the lecturer has chosen to talk about Frank Gehry? What does he say about Gehry in his introduction? Did you hear the phrase "one of my favorite architects"? This tells you how the lecturer views Gehry's work. As you listen to this lecture, think about what the lecturer *doesn't* say about Gehry. A lecturer's point of view will influence the information that you're hearing.

Find audioscript for the other Coaching Tips at www.pearsonlongman.com/contemporarytopics.

Talk about the Topic *page 78*

Qiang: You know, Frank Gehry's work is so cool. All those wild shapes and strange angles? That guy's going to go into the history book as one of the greatest architects ever.

Michael: Hmm. I mean, I can see why you'd say that—his buildings are distinct. But, in my opinion, he'll be forgotten by history.

Qiang: Huh?

Michael: Well, I mean, his work's like bubble gum. You chew it for twenty minutes, and then you're bored with it.

Yhinny: What? I wouldn't say that. Maybe his work might not excite you. But his buildings can be found all over the world—and I mean, come on, they're unlike anything else!

Michael: I mean, I hate to disagree but to me, "different" doesn't mean "good."

May: OK, then what would you say about his engineering abilities—can you say he's noteworthy for that?

Michael: OK, sure, I can see that. But then why doesn't he put those abilities to use in a more practical way, like building bridges?

Yhinny: OK, OK, Mike, so you're the traditionalist.

May: OK, I mean, to tell you the truth, I'm not too crazy about his work either. But I think his . . . I don't know how to say it? Resourcefulness? . . . Is inspiring. I mean, to use old building materials— chain-link fence and plywood—it's so much better than throwing it away.

Qiang: So here's our environmentalist!

Michael: OK, well then what about you two? What are you? I mean, are you traditionalists? Modernists? Or what?

Qiang: I don't know. What are we?

Yhinny: I don't know. I guess you can just call us Frank Gehry enthusiasts!

Michael: Maybe you guys should start a fan club.

Qiang: Maybe we will.

Take the Unit Test

1. Which of these topics does the lecturer *not* discuss?
2. What is the lecture mainly about?
3. What did Vitruvius say about buildings?
4. What is another way to say "the reason" a building is being built?
5. Which principle do architects often disagree about?
6. Why does the speaker mention styles in clothes and cars?
7. Why does the speaker consider Gehry an architectural pioneer?
8. What is using simple building materials and chain-link fence an example of?
9. How are Gehry's designs innovative?
10. Why did Gehry develop his dynamic style?

Extend the Topic *page 80*

Host: Are you interested in living to be a hundred years old or more? If so, these apartments might be the ticket for you. In 2005, nine apartments known as Reversible Destiny Lofts were designed in Tokyo by architects Shusaku Arakawa and Madeline Gins. These architects, like Frank Gehry, challenge traditional ideas about architecture. So what makes these apartments different from other apartments? For starters, each apartment has sloped floors—the floors aren't flat like in most apartments. As a result, the people living there often lose their balance and fall over. They have to work hard just to walk around. Plus, light switches are hidden, and there are no closets. This, of course, makes it very difficult to find things. Why did the architects think this design was a good idea? Well, they've said that it makes people alert. People have to work hard every day just to live there. This keeps their instincts strong, so they'll live better and longer. In other words, these apartments may be the secret to long life. As strange as this may sound, the apartments meet building-code requirements in Tokyo. And, there are plans to build similar apartments in other cities, like Paris. So if you're interested in a long life, check this out. . . .

ANSWER KEY

Build Your Vocabulary *pages 73–74*

A. 1. d 2. b 3. a 4. c 5. e 6. i 7. f 8. g 9. j 10. h
B. Interact with Vocabulary! 1. aesthetics
2. aesthetic, aesthetically 3. distinct 4. distinguish
5. innovator 6. innovative 7. innovation
8. sculpture 9. sculptor

Focus Your Attention *page 75*

A. Signal phrases/cues: I want to tell you the term . . . ;
. . . right?; What about . . . ?; it's important to understand . . . ; Are you with me?; I want to highlight . . . ; Any questions?; Important information: program = the reason a building is built; mosque, church, temple = religious program; theater, sports stadium = entertainment program; specify program so that all working on it keep in mind what it's designed for

Listen for Main Ideas *pages 76–77*

B. 1. b 2. b 3. c 4. a 5. c 6. b

Listen for Details *page 77*

B. 1. T 2. T 3. F (school) 4. F (Not everyone agrees because styles are always changing.) 5. T
6. F (it was practical/at the construction site) 7. F (isn't worried; knows it's structurally sound) 8. T
9. F (more like an artist than an engineer) 10. T

Talk about the Topic *page 78*

A. 1. Michael, May 2. Yhinny, Qiang 3. Michael
4. Michael, May **B.** 1. Disagreeing 2. Disagreeing
3. Asking for opinions or ideas 4. Agreeing
5. Asking for opinions or ideas

Review Your Notes *page 79*

Notes may vary. **I. 3 principles of Vitruvius:**
A. meet its intended use; best design for its purpose; e.g., school; B. be sound; be strong; e.g., withstand bad weather; C. be beautiful; e.g., pleasing to look at and to be in; **II. 3 features of Gehry's style:**
A. resourceful: used sheet metal, plywood; e.g., California mall; B. playful: bright colors, fun designs; e.g., EMP Museum, Seattle; DG Bank, Germany; C. innovative: experimented with new ideas; walls aren't straight, irregular shapes; e.g., Vitra Design Building; **III. Ex.'s of his work:**
Dancing House in Prague; Walt Disney Concert Hall in Los Angeles, Calif.; Fish Dance restaurant in Kobe, Japan; Venice, Calif. store; plus structures mentioned in II.; **IV. Reasons Gehry developed style:** he thinks like an artist; pushes the limits of sound engineering to create beautiful buildings;
V. Reasons speaker likes Gehry: Gehry challenges him to explore new ideas

Take the Unit Test

1. c 2. b 3. d 4. b 5. d 6. b 7. c 8. a 9. d 10. b

 **TEST** ARCHITECTURE: Frank Gehry

 Listen to each question. Circle the letter of the correct answer.

1. a. the three characteristics of architecture

   b. the characteristics of Gehry's work

   c. the reasons styles in architecture change

   d. the reasons Gehry developed his style

2. a. traditional values in architecture

   b. the development of Gehry's style

   c. examples of Gehry's designs

   d. the science of architecture

3. a. They should be sound.

   b. They should meet their intended use.

   c. They should be beautiful.

   d. all of the above

4. a. its style

   b. its intended use

   c. its beauty

   d. its safety

5. a. how to design a building to meet its intended use

   b. how to make a building that's structurally sound

   c. how to make a building that's functional

   d. how to create a building that's aesthetically pleasing

6. a. to emphasize the styles from fifty years ago

   b. to point out that styles in architecture change, too

   c. to point out the styles in architecture in the 1970s

   d. to show how Gehry's style changed

7. a. because Gehry lived in California

   b. because Gehry worked on buildings in many countries

   c. because Gehry wasn't afraid to try new ideas

   d. because Gehry designed the Walt Disney Concert Hall in L.A.

8. a. being resourceful

   b. being artistic

   c. being innovative

   d. being playful

9. a. His neighbors didn't like his house.

   b. Many of his buildings don't have straight walls.

   c. He uses irregular angles and shapes.

   d. both b and c

10. a. because he follows traditional principles of architecture

    b. because he thinks more like an artist, a sculptor

    c. because he builds many types of buildings

    d. because he worked mostly in California in the 1970s

UNIT 9 · PUBLIC HEALTH
Building Immunity

UNIT OVERVIEW

In this unit, students explore factors that contribute to good health. The lecture focuses on immunity, specifically while traveling. Follow-up projects extend the topic to comfort foods, laughter as a way to stay healthy, and research on tips for traveling abroad.

Connect to the Topic *page 82*　　　　　　　　　　　　　　*~10 minutes*

Working in pairs, students read a list of factors that affect their health and add their own ideas. They then answer questions about what they do to stay healthy at home and abroad.

Build Your Vocabulary *pages 83–84*　　　　　　　　　　　　*~15 minutes*

Students study these words and phrases related to public health and immunity:

adapting to	exposed to	recover
back home	from time to time	resist (germs and
based on	immune to	bacteria)
build up resistance to	in more detail	stress
caused by	incidence of (AIDS)	tend to
contagious (disease)	keep from getting sick	transmitted
crucial (to)	microorganisms	vaccine
develop through	promote	

After the Interact with Vocabulary! activity, you may want to have students practice using the boldfaced words with their partners. Knowing collocations can help students expand their vocabularies and increase their fluency.

Focus Your Attention *page 85*　　　　　　　　　　　　　　*~10 minutes*

Students learn cues that lecturers use to show how ideas are connected. These and other examples are provided:

Indicating cause-and-effect relationships
If . . . , then . . .
Because of . . .

Changing topics
I want to mention . . .

Connecting to an earlier idea
Do you recall . . .
Think back to . . .

Returning to the topic
Back to our focus today . . .
Back to (the topic) . . .

Listen to the Lecture *pages 86–87*　　　　　　　　　　　　*~30 minutes*

Prior to listening to the unit lecture on adaptive immunity, students write their own ideas about the health risks of international travel (Before You Listen). They then listen to the lecture and answer multiple-choice questions (Listen for Main Ideas) and sentence completion questions (Listen for Details).
Lecture video time: 6 min. 48 sec.　　　　*Number of episodes: 12*

Talk about the Topic *page 88*

~20 minutes

Four students—Michael, Yhinny, Qiang, and May—discuss the lecture. Part A focuses on matching these students with comments from the discussion. In Part B, your students work on identifying these discussion strategies:

- Asking for opinions or ideas: "But, anyways, what about everyone else?"
- Offering a fact or example: "So, I can tell you from personal experience . . . "
- Paraphrasing: "She said it can take your body two years . . . "

For Part C, students are encouraged to use the discussion strategies they've learned. They may use phrases from the student discussion and/or the Discussion Strategy box, or they may come up with their own.

> **BONUS ACTIVITIES**
>
> For the third topic, have students do additional research on the pros and cons of vaccines, and then have a debate.

Student discussion video time: 1 min. 30 sec.

Review Your Notes *page 89*

~15 minutes

Students focus on reconstructing their notes, paying attention to cause-and-effect relationships.

> **BONUS ACTIVITY**
>
> Have pairs form small groups to compare their information and work together to summarize the key points of the lecture. Remind them to use the discussion strategies they have learned.

Take the Unit Test *Teacher's Pack page 55*

~15 minutes

You may want to play the lecture again before giving the test. Students answer standard test questions about the content of the lecture. Specifically, the test covers the following: adaptive immunity, health challenges of travel, natural versus artificial immunity, and other health considerations.

Extend the Topic *pages 90–91*

~30 minutes

- Listening and Discussion: Students listen to a doctor talk about the merits of comfort foods. Then they discuss what they heard.
- Reading and Discussion: Students learn about and discuss how laughter can boost immunity.
- Research and Presentation: Students choose between health-related travel recommendations and career possibilities within the field of public health. They research their topics and present their findings.

Focus Your Attention:
Try It Out! *page 85*

Speaker: As you know, in the field of public health, we look at basic factors that help make both an individual and a community healthy. Think back to the previous lecture, when you were asked to consider the importance of clean air. If people don't have clean air to breathe, then this can cause many health problems, can't it? Today, I want to talk about another basic factor: clean water. Good water. By this I mean water that is safe to drink. Because access to clean water is a major issue for millions of people worldwide, we need to consider this. If children in particular don't have clean water, it can cause serious health problems. So let's turn to some countries where the lack of clean water is an issue . . . Oh, before I forget, I want to mention there's a good article about children and water in the recent issue of the *Journal of Global Public Health* . . .

Listen for Main Ideas and Listen for Details *pages 86–87*

Public health lecturer: **E1** Hello everyone. We're going to start talking about immunity. The immune system is the system in our body that fights diseases. Its job is to defend us against things that might make us sick—for example, bacteria and viruses. How healthy we are depends on how well we can defend ourselves. At home or traveling, we need a strong immune system in order to be healthy. I became very interested in this topic while I was doing research in Africa. I had studied immunity in school, but living in another country helped me understand the issues much better. **E2** Today I'm going to focus on adaptive immunity. I'll explain this in detail in a minute. But first know that there are different kinds of adaptive immunity. We develop it naturally based on where we live, and based on some diseases we get. We can also develop it artificially through vaccines. OK? **E3** Basically, adaptive immunity means that our bodies learn to fight things that we're exposed to. If you live in Tokyo, you'll develop adaptive immunity to the microorganisms in Tokyo. Similarly, someone in Paris develops immunity to the germs in Paris, in Beijing, immunity to what's in Beijing—OK? You could pick any place. Our bodies adapt—they adjust—to what's in our environment. Building up adaptive immunity takes time; it can take a couple of years. This is the reason why young children, say, one to three years old, get sick often. They haven't built up the resistance to the germs around them. As they get older, they tend to get sick

less. **E4** Let's consider what happens when someone travels to another country. For example, a Chinese business traveler goes to South Africa, or an American student goes to Ecuador. The germs and diseases are different there. The adaptive immunity these two individuals have developed back home won't protect them abroad, will it? Well, what's the result? They're more likely to get sick. And it may not just affect them. Let's suppose that the business traveler is exposed to a contagious disease, like influenza, and she becomes sick after she returns home. She might spread it to someone back home—someone who, most likely, lacks the immunity to that influenza virus. Public health officials are very aware of how quickly contagious diseases can spread. We're all concerned about serious diseases like avian—or bird—flu, as well as less serious viruses and germs. With so much global travel these days, there are more incidents of diseases being transmitted. So, we need to keep in mind the immunity issues related to global travel. **E5** Now let's look at two types of adaptive immunity in more detail. I'll give you an example of each. Please pay attention to how they're different. First of all, there's a girl named Kimi who catches a cold. In a week, she feels much better. The adaptive immunity made her body strong enough to resist the cold virus that made her sick this time, so she got well. That doesn't mean that she'll never get a cold again, does it? We all get colds from time to time. **E6** Now, let's consider Kimi's younger sister, Meg. Meg catches the chicken pox virus, right? A common childhood disease, caused by a virus, the VZV virus. After ten days, she recovers. She shouldn't get chicken pox ever again, not for the rest of her life. We call this life-long protective immunity. **E7** In both cases we see adaptive immunity at work. Here's the crucial difference: Our immune systems only "remember" certain viruses. So, Kimi is not immune to all cold viruses. She'll get a cold again in her life. But, Meg's body has what we call immunological memory to chicken pox. Her immune system will "remember" chicken pox and she won't get it again. She has life-long protective immunity. **E8** I want to move on now to talking about vaccines. Vaccines are one of the most effective ways to prevent certain types of disease. The idea behind vaccines is simple: It is better to keep people from getting sick than to try to treat them after they've already become sick. **E9** Do you recall from your book how vaccines work? In brief: A vaccine puts something into your body that your immune system responds to as "foreign." The immune system fights that "foreign body," and creates antibodies against it to protect you in the future. Think back to Meg and her chicken pox, and her immunological memory. It's a similar situation here with vaccines. Your immune system "remembers" something from the vaccine, and now knows how to fight back to prevent you from getting sick. E10 Vaccines are a very convenient, quick way to boost our immunity. Doctors recommend vaccines before we go to other countries because there isn't time for our bodies to adjust to the germs in the short time we're there. I just have to add a quick comment. Some people in the developed countries like the U.S. don't give their kids vaccines because they believe they're unnecessary and harmful. Personally, I think that's irresponsible. I know from my own research in Africa that vaccines for young children can make a huge, positive difference in a community's health. Anyway, moving on. E11 Now let's briefly consider some positive steps that we can take to promote our own immune systems and good health in general. First, I'd say good nutrition. What we eat is very important to our overall health. Malnutrition is the most common reason for immunity problems worldwide. Second: Keep things clean. Basic hygiene. Our hands, our homes, everything needs to be clean. Third: Reduce stress. That's a big one. Stress affects everyone, young and old. It can lower our immunity. E12 To sum up the key points of today: Think about what adaptive immunity is, and how we can develop it. And consider what you can do to stay healthy.

Coaching Tips

[1] Critical Thinking: Identifying point of view
Here we learn that the speaker did research in Africa, where she learned about public health issues related to immunity. By sharing this background information, the speaker establishes her credibility, or her authority on the subject. She's also indicating a point of view—an opinion on the subject of immunity and its importance to the public's health. As you listen to a lecture, you can note in the margins comments that indicate a lecturer's opinion. *Find audioscript for the other Coaching Tips at www.pearsonlongman.com/contemporarytopics.*

Talk about the Topic *page 88*

Michael: So, I can tell you from personal experience about the importance of adaptive immunity.

May: Why? What happened?

Michael: Well, last year, I was on this study abroad program where you travel around the world by ship, stopping in different countries, studying cultures. I mean, it was great but every new country we stopped in, I seemed to get a new cold!

Qiang: Wow, that's too bad. So, your body didn't learn to adapt to the germs, huh?

Michael: Well, we only stopped in one place for a few days.

Yhinny: Yeah, and she said it can take your body two years to learn to fight off some microorganisms.

Qiang: And what about stress—was that a factor for you?

Michael: Definitely. I mean, making all new friends, you know, seeing new places—it was fun, but stressful.

Qiang: Hmm.

May: What about your diet?

Michael: Well, actually, we stopped in places like Japan and Tunisia and Jamaica—so I ate like a king! . . . But, anyways, what about everyone else?

Yhinny: Well, my parents, they're completely against vaccines. I've never had them.

May: Wow, the lecturer would not agree with that decision!

Yhinny: I know. But my parents believe that vaccines actually do more harm than good. That your body's immunity is best, especially if you live in places where there're fewer contagious diseases.

Qiang: So you're like a living example of adaptive immunity, huh?

Yhinny: Yeah, I've been lucky. And, I should tell you all—I'm a total clean freak, so probably that's helped!

Qiang: Yeah.

May: I'm sure.

Qiang: Yeah totally.

Michael: I can see that.

Take the Unit Test

1. What is the main topic of the lecture?
2. Which of the following topics does the lecturer *not* discuss?
3. The lecturer says, "Our bodies adapt—they adjust—to what's in our environment." What does this mean?
4. Why do many very young children get sick a lot?
5. A businessman gets sick with influenza in Paris. After he returns home to Korea, his family gets sick. Why? Choose *two* answers.
6. If you catch a cold, you'll probably recover in about a week. Why?
7. Why do people who get the chicken pox then develop life-long immunity?
8. Which of the following statements does *not* reflect the lecturer's attitude toward vaccines?
9. What connection does the lecturer make between illnesses like the chicken pox and vaccines?
10. Which statement best summarizes the speaker's attitude toward staying healthy?

Extend the Topic *page 90*

Talk show host: Well, everyone gets a cold at some time. There are more than 200 viruses that can cause a cold, so they're pretty hard to avoid altogether. So what can we do if we get one? That's the question for our guest today, Dr. Michelle Diego. Welcome.

Dr. Diego: Thanks. Good to be here.

Talk show host: So let's start with the expression "Feed a cold, starve a fever." Is this really good advice?

Dr. Diego: Most experts say no. Instead, listen to your body. Eat if you feel hungry, but we don't need to eat a lot. When we're sick, many of us only want simple comfort foods—like soup, for example. In fact, studies show that chicken soup can actually help clear your head and help you breathe more easily. Add a little ginger, or hot sauce, and it'll work even better!

Talk show host: Wow.

Dr. Diego: Or hot tea. Hot tea with lemon and honey. Even a bowl of simple, warm rice. Or, a cookie or two, like your grandmother or mother used to bake!

Talk show host: Mmm. Yum.

Dr. Diego: In fact, some doctors, myself included, say that comfort foods—foods that make us feel soothed just by eating them—that comfort foods may be the secret to getting well faster. We get sick when we're out of balance. And a little comfort from our food may help us recover more quickly!

Talk show host: Cookies, huh? I'm still thinking about those cookies you mentioned . . .

ANSWER KEY

Build Your Vocabulary *pages 83–84*

A. 1. a 2. c 3. b 4. f 5. d 6. e 7. g 8. i 9. h 10. k 11. j 12. l **B. Interact with Vocabulary!** 1. back 2. on 3. through 4. by 5. up, to 6. to 7. in 8. from, to 9. to 10. from

Focus Your Attention *page 85*

A. phrases: Think back to . . . ; If people . . . then/this can cause . . . ; Because access . . . we need to . . . ; If children . . . it can cause . . .

Listen for Main Ideas *page 86*

B. 1. a 2. b 3. c 4. b 5. c 6. b

Listen for Details *page 87*

B. 1. strong 2. Africa 3. immunity 4. more 5. isn't 6. avian flu 7. will 8. won't 9. keep people from getting sick 10. Stress

Talk about the Topic *page 88*

A. 1. Michael 2. Qiang 3. May 4. Yhinny
B. 1. Offering a fact or example 2. Paraphrasing 3. Asking for opinions or ideas 4. Asking for opinions or ideas

Review Your Notes *page 89*

Answers will vary: **If you have a strong** . . . to resist viruses, stay healthy, recover more quickly. **If you live** . . . develop immunity to the germs there, don't develop immunity to the germs in other places; **Young children** . . . get sicker more often, need vaccines; **Doctors recommend** . . . our immune systems aren't ready for other germs, public health is endangered if we don't

Take the Unit Test

1. b 2. a 3. c 4. d 5. b and c 6. a 7. a 8. a 9. c 10. b

PUBLIC HEALTH: Building Immunity

UNIT 9 TEST

Listen to each question. Circle the letter of the correct answer.

1. a. contagious diseases
   b. adaptive immunity
   c. healthy lifestyles
   d. basic hygiene

2. a. various types of vaccines
   b. risks of foreign travel
   c. types of adaptive immunity
   d. how we develop adaptive immunity

3. a. We need a strong immune system.
   b. We need to fight germs that can harm us.
   c. We develop immunity to what we're exposed to.
   d. There are many microorganisms that can make us sick.

4. a. because they tend to get sick often
   b. because they can defend themselves against harmful bacteria and viruses
   c. because they have stronger immune systems
   d. because they haven't yet built up resistance to the germs around them

5. a. because there are many viruses
   b. because contagious diseases can be transmitted globally
   c. because the family's adaptive immunity didn't protect them
   d. because it's more important to stay in your home country

6. a. because your immune system will eventually fight off the virus
   b. because you are immune to the virus
   c. because you feel better
   d. because your body has immunological memory

7. a. because their body "recognizes" the VZV virus the next time they're exposed
   b. because it's a contagious disease
   c. because they don't have immunological memory
   d. because it's a childhood disease

8. a. They're irresponsible.
   b. They're very convenient.
   c. They're very effective.
   d. They're very fast.

9. a. They both require a strong immune system.
   b. They both prevent us from getting sick.
   c. They both create an immunological memory.
   d. They each boost immunity quickly.

10. a. We should not travel as much.
    b. We need to be aware of the risks and take steps to stay healthy.
    c. Adaptive immunity ensures that we will stay healthy.
    d. We have little control over staying healthy.

TEACHING TIPS

UNIT OVERVIEW

In this unit, students explore the principles of good journalism. The lecture focuses on seven principles outlined by the Committee of Concerned Journalists, an international organization, and the impact of the Internet on journalism. Follow-up projects extend the topic to the role of local newspapers in developing a sense of community, the rise of celebrity news in the media, and the assessment of a current news story or website.

Connect to the Topic   *page 92*   *~10 minutes*

Students take a survey about their media habits. Survey questions concern how students know what's going on and their attitudes toward fairness and bias in the media. They compare responses with a partner.

Build Your Vocabulary   *pages 93–94*   *~15 minutes*

Students study these words and phrases related to media studies and journalistic principles:

(cover the story) adequately	extensions of	professional
balance of	kinds of media	relevant to
biased toward	multiple	report on
compiled	multiple sources	underlying (principles of)
compiled by	objective	understanding of
covered	obligation	version of
ethics	paradigm	

For the Interact with Vocabulary! activity, you may want to encourage students to notice the boldfaced word in each sentence. When paired with the correct particle from the second column, these words form collocations, which are valuable in building students' vocabulary and fluency.

Focus Your Attention   *page 95*   *~10 minutes*

Students learn that one way lecturers organize their information is by enumerating and repeating key phrases. Students also hear how speakers indicate the end of a topic. Examples like the following are provided:

*Today I'm going to talk about **three characteristics of a good news website**.*
Characteristic 1: A good news website . . .
Characteristic 2: A good news website . . .
Now I want to turn to . . .

Listen to the Lecture   *pages 96–97*   *~30 minutes*

Prior to listening to the unit lecture on journalism, students write their own ideas about what makes someone a good journalist (Before You Listen). Students then listen to the lecture and answer multiple-choice questions (Listen for Main Ideas) and sentence completion questions (Listen for Details).

Lecture video time: 6 min. 54 sec.   *Number of episodes: 10*

NOTE

Remember that with the DVD, you can play the lecture in different modes: video, video with subtitles, video with Coaching Tips, video with Presentation Points, video with Coaching Tips and subtitles, and video with Coaching Tips and Presentation Points. (We do not recommend playing the video with both the Presentation Points and subtitles on.) Note that while the DVD is compatible with most computer media players, for optimum viewing we suggest playing the DVD on a television using a DVD player. You can also play the lecture as audio only, using the CD.

Talk about the Topic *page 98*   *~20 minutes*

Four students—Molly, Rob, Alana, and Ayman—discuss the lecture. Part A focuses on matching students with ideas from the discussion. In Part B, students work on identifying these discussion strategies:

- Expressing an opinion: "Even some 'journalists' don't tell the whole truth."
- Agreeing: "Yeah, exactly."
- Paraphrasing: "What she means is . . . "

For Part C, students are encouraged to use the discussion strategies they've learned. They may use phrases from the student discussion and/or the Discussion Strategy box, or they may come up with their own. For the first discussion topic, you might suggest having students read blog entries on a current news item and summarize in groups the opinions they found.
Student discussion video time: 1 min. 29 sec.

Review Your Notes *page 99*   *~15 minutes*

Students focus on reconstructing their notes, paying attention to facts and opinions.

BONUS ACTIVITY

You can supplement this activity by having students find news stories in the media, identify both facts and opinions, and report their findings to the class.

Take the Unit Test *Teacher's Pack page 61*   *~15 minutes*

You may want to play the lecture again before giving the test. Students answer standard test questions about the content of the lecture. Specifically, the test covers the following: principles of good journalism, the impact of the Internet on journalism, citizen versus professional journalists, and the future of journalism.

Extend the Topic *pages 100–101*   *~30 minutes*

- Listening and Discussion: Students listen to and discuss an extract from a city council meeting on why the local newspaper is important.
- Reading and Discussion: The reading and questions focus on the value of celebrity journalism.
- Research and Presentation: The research project focuses on evaluating the balance of a news story or the content of a community website.

AUDIOSCRIPT

Focus Your Attention: Try It Out! *page 95*

Speaker: OK, so today I'm going to cover the four basic parts of a news story. The first part is called the lede, that's l-e-d-e. The lede is what draws your readers into the story. Two quick examples for you. Example one, the straight lede: "Two men have been arrested in connection with a series of burglaries . . ." Dot dot dot. And example two, the anecdotal lede: "Dolores Calva's insurance will replace the laptop and other items recently burgled from her apartment. But the policy doesn't cover peace of mind, the twenty-nine-year-old graduate student only half jokes. . . ." Blah blah blah. OK, after the lede comes what's called the "nut graph." This is the second part of a news story. Here we're told the story's significance—why we should care about this story. All right? OK, the third part of a news story is the body. The body is where sources are quoted and more details are provided. The body is also where, if necessary, "back story" comes in . . .

Listen for Main Ideas and Listen for Details *pages 96–97*

Media studies lecturer: **E1** Today we're going to look at the principles of good journalism. As we all know, there are many different media sources: newspapers, magazines, TV, radio, the Internet. Regardless of the media we work in, as journalists we need to think about the underlying principles of good journalism. Today I'm going to present seven principles compiled by the Committee of Concerned Journalists, a group of more than 7,000 journalists from around the globe. They spent five years doing research to get a deep understanding of what defines good journalism. First, I'll go over these principles. Then we'll consider them in relationship to the Internet because of its growing influence on journalism. **E2** All right, let's get started. Principle 1: Journalists need to tell the truth. We need to verify facts and make clear the sources of our information so that the public can judge for itself what news to trust. They expect us to tell the truth. Principle 2: Journalists' first obligation is to the public, not to advertisers or the owners of the news media. Our job is to keep people informed. Our news stories shouldn't be biased toward the political views or political interests of the owners or sponsors. **E3** Principle 3: Journalists need to be independent and objective. To best do this, we need to use multiple sources of information so that we can provide accurate information and cover all sides of

the story. For example, let's say the government passes stricter laws for teenage drivers. A good reporter needs to get reactions from all sides—government officials, parents, police, teenagers—to cover the story adequately. Otherwise the story may be one-sided. **E4** Principle 4: Be watchdogs. We must provide the public with news about important government actions that affect them—for example, a decision to raise taxes. In a democracy, citizens need to know they can rely on journalists to let them know what's happening in government. **E5** That takes us to Principle 5: A journalist must be a good storyteller. We must ask ourselves what news is most relevant to the public, and then tell our news stories in an interesting way. The committee calls this "storytelling with a purpose." **E6** Principle 6: Every journalist needs to be honest and have a sense of ethics and responsibility. We need to think for ourselves and take a stand for what we believe in, professionally speaking. But this is sometimes difficult to do, especially if the company we are working for encourages or discourages coverage of a particular issue. **E7** Principle 7: Keep the news balanced. Cover both good and bad news in order to provide a complete picture of what's going on in the community. People want to know about terrible crimes, but also about successful literacy programs and great concerts. **E8** Now I want to turn to the role of the Internet. No one in journalism can dispute its impact. Back when I started out as a journalist, there was no Internet, which you probably find hard to imagine. Let's look at some of the ways it has changed journalism. First is how most journalists conduct their research. According to the executive director for the Committee of Concerned Journalists, "The Internet has given journalists huge opportunities to cover more stories, and to cover them in a different way than traditional media have done." Different indeed. These days many reporters rarely leave their offices. They use the Internet, e-mail, and the phone instead of conducting live interviews or going to the scene of the event. **E9** Another impact of the Internet has been an increased number of the official news outlets in the form of websites. However, many Internet sites are just extensions of existing news media—television news networks, various news publications—and feature the same journalists' stories rather than additional stories. Finally, Internet blogs have had a significant impact on modern journalism. Blogs provide a way for what we call "citizen journalists" to report their own version of the news. Think about it. Traditionally, professional journalists have decided what news to report to the public. Now, through blogs, "citizen journalists" are deciding what's important. **E10** So, what do all of these changes mean for the future of journalism? Well, I don't think professional journalists will become extinct, like dinosaurs. Rather, I see a new paradigm for journalism; a partnership between "citizen journalists" and professional journalists. There's room for all of us. That said, we all must be committed to the seven principles. And that's where I'm going to leave off today. Please discuss in your study groups which of the seven principles you think are more valuable to good journalism.

Coaching Tips

[1] Note-taking: Using abbreviations and symbols
Did you catch all of that information? The speaker gave a lot of numbers and facts in a short amount of time. Using abbreviations and symbols is one way to write information quickly. Here are examples of some abbreviations and symbols you could use: [see video for note-taking example].

Find audioscript for the other Coaching Tips at www.pearsonlongman.com/contemporarytopics.

Talk about the Topic *page 98*

Alana: Well, this lecture was interesting for me, because I want to be a journalist.

Molly: Really?

Alana: Yeah.

Ayman: Yeah, you'd be a good journalist.

Alana: Yeah, I mean, everyone tells me that I'm a good storyteller.

Rob: Oh yeah, but, come on—journalism isn't storytelling. Journalism is about reporting the facts!

Molly: No, no, no—what she means is she has the talent for making something interesting.

Alana: Yeah, exactly. Remember? It's Principle 5: "We must tell our news stories in an interesting way."

Rob: Sorry—I guess I missed that one.

Ayman: You know which one I didn't understand? The one about balance. What does that mean?

Rob: Oh, well, all right, think about your local TV news, and how every night they just report the same things—it's car accidents and deaths, and crime. Just the same stuff over and over again.

Molly: I hate TV news. I believe you, you have to find the balance yourself, you know? Looking on the Internet, reading magazines, listening to the radio.

Alana: That's what I like about blogs. They let you see a different side of (a) story than you usually can find in a traditional media.

Ayman: But doesn't it bother you they're just bloggers—I mean, not real journalists? How, how do you trust that you're getting the truth?

Alana: You know, even some "journalists" don't tell the whole truth. Like those on political channels.

Molly: Hello! Now those are the real storytellers!

Rob: Tell me about it!

Molly: I just don't believe a word that they say anymore.

Rob: You can't, you can't anymore!

Molly: I mean no, I think they're just . . .

Rob: It's more entertainment!

Take the Unit Test

1. What is the lecture mainly about?
2. Which topic does the lecturer *not* mention?
3. Why do journalists need to make clear their sources of information? Choose *two* answers.
4. The lecturer says, "Journalists' first obligation is to the public." What does this mean?
5. Why is it important for journalists to use multiple sources?
6. Why do journalists need to pay attention to what the government is doing?
7. The lecturer refers to "storytelling with a purpose." What does she mean by this?
8. Which one of the following statements does *not* reflect the lecturer's attitude about the Internet's impact on journalism?
9. What is the lecturer's main point about blogs?
10. Which statement reflects the lecturer's attitude about citizen and professional journalists?

Extend the Topic *page 100*

Mayor: Next we'll hear from the Millers, owners of the *Lakeville Ledger.*

Mrs. Miller: Thank you, mayor. We're here this evening to make some special requests. As you know, my husband and I own and operate the local newspaper, circulation about 2,000 . . .

Mr. Miller: And dropping. Mayor, council members, as owners of the paper, I and my wife are here to appeal to the people of Lakeville for help. Our readership is dropping, and if the *Lakeville Ledger* dies, well, then . . .

Mrs. Miller: . . . We're concerned that Lakeville's sense of community could die along with it.

Mayor: What's caused this decline in readership?

Mrs. Miller: The Internet, namely. I mean, there are of course still people out there who enjoy a "real" newspaper with their morning cup of coffee. But increasingly, people are choosing the quick, free option of just reading headlines on their computer.

Mr. Miller: So, our first request is the city's permission to add newspaper distribution boxes throughout downtown. We only have two currently.

Mrs. Miller: And we'll be launching a website in a few months, basically an online version of the paper. And we'd like to include a link to the city's website, and vice versa.

Mayor: Interesting. Council members, any questions? . . .

Build Your Vocabulary *pages 93–94*

A. 1. enough for a particular purpose 2. put together from different sources 3. reported the details of a news event 4. rules about what is right and wrong 5. many 6. not influenced by one's own beliefs 7. duty 8. model or approach 9. trained to do a job for money 10. basic, fundamental **B.** 1. underlying ethic, profession 2. obligation 3. compiled 4. paradigm, cover 5. adequate, multiple 6. objective **C. Interact with Vocabulary!** 1. a 2. c 3. d 4. b 5. e 6. h 7. j 8. g 9. i 10. f

Focus Your Attention *page 95*

A. . . . the four basic parts of a news story. The first part is called . . . Two quick examples . . . Example one . . . example two . . . is the second part of a news story. . . . the third part of a new story is . . .

Listen for Main Ideas *page 96*

B. 1. c 2. a and c 3. a 4. b 5. c

Listen for Details *page 97*

B. 1. five 2. all media 3. tell the truth 4. the public 5. the government 6. interesting 7. a complete picture of what's going on in their community 8. in their offices 9. have not 10. blogs

Talk about the Topic *page 98*

Suggested answers: **A.** 1. Rob 2. Molly, Alana 3. Molly 4. Alana **B.** 1. Paraphrasing 2. Agreeing 3. Expressing an opinion 4. Agreeing and Expressing an opinion 5. Agreeing

Review Your Notes *page 99*

7 principles: 1. tell the truth 2. first obligation is to the public, not the owner of the media outlet 3. need to be independent and objective 4. provide the public with information about government actions that affect them 5. be a good storyteller: storytelling with a purpose 6. be honest and have a strong sense of ethics 7. balance the news, good and bad; give a complete picture of what's going on; **Impact of Internet:** how research is done—more news websites, blogs, citizen journalists; **citizen vs. professional journalists:** Now anyone can decide what to write about; **speaker's point of view:** Speaker thinks room for both citizen and professional journalists, but all must follow 7 principles of good journalism

Take the Unit Test

1. b 2. d 3. a and c 4. d 5. c 6. a 7. b 8. c 9. a 10. c

MEDIA STUDIES: Principles of Journalism

 Listen to each question. Circle the letter of the correct answer.

1. a. the types of stories the public finds most interesting
   b. the underlying principles of good journalism
   c. techniques for presenting all sides of a story
   d. both a and c

2. a. the various media sources people use every day
   b. blogs on the Internet
   c. the impact of the Internet on journalism
   d. the reasons many people prefer electronic media

3. a. because the public wants to judge for itself what news to trust
   b. because the public isn't informed about some events
   c. so that the public can determine if journalists are telling the truth
   d. because the public doesn't always pay attention to what's going on

4. a. Journalists need to check their sources of information.
   b. Journalists need to consider the financial interests of the owners.
   c. Journalists should consider the advertisers of the news media they work for.
   d. Journalists shouldn't be biased toward the owners of the news media they work for.

5. a. because they need to be objective
   b. because advertising depends on it
   c. because they need to cover all sides of a story
   d. because more sources make stories more interesting

6. a. because citizens rely on journalists to keep them informed
   b. because journalists need to cover all sides of a story
   c. because the news should be balanced
   d. because the news should be accurate

7. a. keeping the news balanced
   b. telling the most relevant news in an interesting way
   c. deciding which side of the story to tell
   d. deciding which information is accurate

8. a. It's changed how journalists conduct research.
   b. It's helped journalists gather important information.
   c. It's significantly increased the number of stories available to the public.
   d. It's improved the news coverage because the same journalists are writing the stories.

9. a. Citizen journalists are now also deciding what news is important.
   b. Only professional journalists should decide what news to report.
   c. Citizen journalists' news stories aren't accurate.
   d. Ordinary citizens don't understand news events very well.

10. a. The field of professional journalism is in trouble.
    b. Professional journalism needs to change.
    c. Everyone needs to follow the principles of good journalism.
    d. Internet news sites are increasing rapidly.

BIOLOGY
DNA Testing

UNIT 11

TEACHING TIPS

UNIT OVERVIEW

In this unit, students will explore some applications of DNA testing, as well as related ethical and privacy issues. The lecture focuses on the processes of creating a DNA fingerprint and using it in a crime lab. It also provides an overview of two medical uses of DNA testing. Follow-up projects extend the topic to other applications of DNA testing.

Connect to the Topic *page 102*   *~10 minutes*

Students complete a chart about themselves and their families. The chart concerns physical characteristics as well as personality traits, talents, and diseases. Students discuss their charts with a partner.

Build Your Vocabulary *pages 103–104*   *~15 minutes*

Students study these words and phrases related to biology and DNA testing:

access to	end up with	match between
at risk for	extract (DNA)	medical (field)
at the crime scene	for one of two	pros and cons of
combination of	reasons	revealed
concentrated on	identical (twins)	statistically
concerns about	linked to	traits (passed down)
diagnose	match	used by

After the Interact with Vocabulary! activity, you may want to have students practice using the boldfaced words with their partners. Knowing collocations can help students expand their vocabularies and increase their fluency.

Focus Your Attention *page 105*   *~10 minutes*

Students learn signal words and phrases that lecturers use to describe a process. They learn how to put their notes into graphic organizers based on these signals:

They start by . . .	*Next . . .*	*And then . . .*
First . . .	*Then . . .*	*At that point . . .*
	After that . . .	*Finally . . .*

Listen to the Lecture *pages 106–107*   *~30 minutes*

Prior to listening to the unit lecture on some uses of DNA testing, students write down their own ideas about how DNA testing is used (Before You Listen). Students then listen to the lecture and answer multiple-choice questions (Listen for Main Ideas) and true/false questions (Listen for Details).

Lecture video time: 7 min. 15 sec.   *Number of episodes: 10*

Talk about the Topic *page 108*

~20 minutes

Four students—Hannah, River, Manny, and Mia—discuss the lecture. Part A focuses on matching these students with ideas from the discussion. In Part B, your students work on identifying these discussion strategies:

- Expressing an opinion: "Yeah, isn't she great?"
- Disagreeing: "Come on. That's not true."
- Keeping the discussion on topic: "Hey . . . back to DNA, OK?"

For Part C, students are encouraged to use the discussion strategies they've learned. They may use phrases from the student discussion, or they may come up with their own.

BONUS ACTIVITIES

In addition to discussing the first two topics, some students might like to hold a debate on privacy issues. Encourage them to work in groups to brainstorm ideas and details to support their points of view.

As an extension of the third topic, have students research the Innocence Project and find examples of prison inmates freed from prison for crimes they didn't commit because of DNA testing.

Student discussion video time: 1 min. 27 sec.

Review Your Notes *page 109*

~15 minutes

Students focus on reconstructing their notes, paying attention to the processes described in the lecture.

Take the Unit Test *Teacher's Pack page 67*

~15 minutes

You may want to play the lecture again before giving the test. Students answer standard test questions about the content of the lecture. Specifically, the test covers the following: the process of creating a DNA fingerprint, the process used in crime labs, medical uses of DNA testing, the relationship between genetic disorders and disease, and privacy questions.

Extend the Topic *pages 110–111*

~30 minutes

- Listening and Discussion: Students hear a sports collector talk about the value of synthetic DNA in marking sports memorabilia, which leads to a discussion on buying authentic versus "knock-off" products.
- Reading and Discussion: Students read about and discuss the discovery of a frozen, 500-year-old body and the use of DNA testing to determine her family lineage.
- Research and Presentation: The project gives students an opportunity to research another application of DNA testing, including the "tagging" of products and the Frozen Ark project, which stores DNA samples of endangered animals worldwide.

Focus Your Attention:
Try It Out! *page 105*

Speaker: So, let's say the police need to know if two people are brother and sister. What do they do? Well, they first conduct DNA testing on one of them, and then conduct DNA testing on the other one. Next, they compare the results and look for genetic similarities. After that, they draw some conclusions about whether the two people are, in fact, brother and sister, since siblings share some of the same genetic information. If they don't share any genetic information, they're obviously not brother and sister, are they? . . .

Listen for Main Ideas and Listen for Details *pages 106–107*

Biology lecturer: **E1** Hello. Today I'd like us to concentrate on DNA. We'll focus on DNA testing— and specifically on DNA testing of people. **E2** Before I explain how it's done, I want to review a bit from the reading. Now, you'll recall that cells comprise every part of our body. Our DNA is in every cell. DNA contains genetic information like eye color, hair color, height, and many other traits passed down from a mother and a father to their child. So, each of us has our own DNA—our own combination of genetic information from our parents. For example, a brother and a sister may end up with the same color of eyes and hair. However, other genetic information received from the parents will be different, which is why they look different. For example, maybe the brother is short like the mother, and the sister is tall like the father. Keep in mind that DNA is in every cell in the body, and that all of these cells contain the same genetic information. **E3** Now, let's look at how DNA testing is used to identify people. Scientists create a DNA profile, also called a DNA "fingerprint." To do this, they need DNA from the person. They take samples from different parts of the body—like hair, blood, skin, fingernails, and body fluids. Next, they extract the DNA from the cells in these samples. Then they read the DNA with a computer. They use the data to create the DNA fingerprint. Statistically, it is very unlikely that any two people will have identical fingerprints. **E4** Now let's ask, how is DNA testing used? Well, there are many ways—for example, to identify an unknown accident victim, or to find out who the father of a child is. Now, here's an interesting one. In 1999, scientists used DNA testing to prove that the son of the French king, Louis the Sixteenth, and Marie-Antoinette in fact died in

prison—he didn't escape as some people had believed. DNA testing identified the son's body. People had been arguing about this for more than two centuries! **E5** Another use of DNA testing is by police to solve crimes. For example, say there's a murder. The police have a suspect they think did it. In the crime lab, scientists use DNA samples from the suspect and DNA samples from the evidence at the crime scene. Then they design what's called probes. When the probes are put in with the DNA samples from the suspect and the DNA samples from the evidence, the probes show if the two sets of samples match. **E6** DNA identification is very effective, but not 100 percent foolproof. For example, suppose the only evidence at the crime scene is blood from the suspect. If there's a match between a sample of the crime scene blood and the suspect's blood, this will help the police. However, a single match—from just blood, in this case—isn't very strong evidence. In contrast, let's say the crime lab has four samples from the crime scene and four samples from the suspect—hair, blood, fingernails, and skin samples. They design four probes, one for each sample, and they get four matches—bingo! The police can now feel more confident that they have the right suspect. Why? Remember, I said DNA is in every cell in our body, and each cell contains all of our unique genetic information. **E7** Now, let's turn to how DNA testing is used in the medical field. Here, let's consider how genetics is being used to diagnose diseases. With diseases, most DNA tests are given for one of two reasons: either to find out if someone has a certain disease, or to see if the person is at risk for developing it. **E8** Researchers have found more than 6,000 genetic disorders. A genetic disorder means something isn't normal in the person's genes: a mutation. A change in one gene can cause a disease. And a DNA test can show if someone has a mutation in a gene that puts them at risk for the disease. Notice I'm not saying that a change in one gene will cause a disease, only that the risk is higher. We're learning more and more every day about genetic diseases. For example, it now appears that the disease Alzheimer's, which damages memory in older people, is linked to our genes. **E9** So, we have to ask: What are the pros and cons of DNA testing in medicine? On the positive side, testing might save lives. If a doctor can diagnose a disease in its early stages, the patient can get treated earlier. Or if a couple wants to have a baby, they can use DNA testing to find out beforehand if any risks for problems or diseases exist. On the negative side, there's the issue of fairness. What happens if DNA testing reveals that we have a genetic disorder that could cause a disease and that information becomes known? **E10** This brings us to some concerns about privacy. A DNA profile contains a lot of personal information. So I'd like you to think about the following questions: One: Who should own the DNA fingerprint once it's made? Two: Who should have access to it? Three: How should genetic information be used? And four: Would you want people, especially people you don't know, to have access to your DNA fingerprint? These are some of the ethical questions we face about how to use the scientific knowledge we have. So, please give these questions some thought as you review the lecture. That's all for now.

Coaching Tips

[1] Critical Thinking: Applying knowledge How much do you know about DNA testing at this point in the lecture? Not much. From past studies or experiences you may know something about genetics or how a person carries the traits of their parents. By applying knowledge you already have, you can get a better understanding of new information. You may even want to add notes of your own to the information a lecturer is giving.
Find audioscript for the other Coaching Tips at www.pearsonlongman.com/contemporarytopics.

Talk about the Topic *page 108*

Mia: You guys know the part of the lecture on DNA profiling? It totally reminded me of this movie that I saw last weekend—this murder mystery . . .

Manny: Oh, the one with Jodie Foster? I love her!

River: Yeah, isn't she great? Have you seen her in *Silence of the Lambs*? She is . . .

Hannah: Hey, hey! Sorry guys—that's interesting. But that's not really why we're here. We're supposed to consider the pros and cons of DNA testing.

River: Oh, right. Well, in my opinion, I mean, it doesn't really matter. Doctors, the government, they already have all your personal information anyway.

Manny: Come on. That's not true. If I have a DNA test, it's nobody's business but my own.

Hannah: Well, I do think sometimes that it's good information for the police to have access to, like in the example of crime.

Mia: I agree. Did you guys see the documentary about that guy who got freed after like twenty years in prison because his DNA didn't match the evidence at the crime scene? I think it's called *Freed*.

Manny: You watch a lot of films don't you?

Hannah: Hey!

Mia: But they're good films!

Hannah: Hey . . . Back to DNA, OK?

Manny: Sorry! OK. Here's my fear: What if I learn from a DNA test that I'm at risk for some disease—

but it's not for sure. What then? I'm supposed to spend my whole life worrying about it?

River: I think you're going to spend your whole life worrying about something anyway.

Mia: I think we're all going to worry about something.

Take the Unit Test

1. What is the main focus of the lecture?
2. Which of these topics does the speaker *not* discuss?
3. What do you think is probably true about a brother who is short and a sister who is tall?
4. To create a DNA fingerprint, scientists first take samples from different parts of the body. What's the next step?
5. Listen to this excerpt from the lecture: "Statistically, it is very unlikely that any two people will have identical fingerprints." Why does the speaker say this?
6. What is identifying an accident victim an example of?
7. In a crime lab, why do scientists need DNA samples from both the suspect and the crime scene?
8. Why is it better to have four DNA matches than one?
9. What causes more than 6,000 genetic disorders?
10. Which of the following is *not* mentioned as a privacy concern?

Extend the Topic *page 110*

Collector: For years I've been a sports collector. I've got baseball cards, Olympic souvenirs. I've even got a few Super Bowl footballs. And you know what I like? That I can finally make sure that these are the real thing before I buy them. How? DNA testing. They now use a little bit of synthetic DNA to mark the footballs, for example. Same for the signed baseball cards. And the Olympic souvenirs? Bags, hats, shirts, whatever—they mark these items with a little bit of special ink. You can't see the mark, but it shows up when a special laser is used. So, now people can know if something is authentic or not. If it doesn't have the mark, it's not authentic. We don't have to worry about wasting our money. Great stuff! So DNA testing can tell you if you have the real thing—or a knock-off. And as any serious collector knows, there's nothing worse than getting stuck with a fake!

ANSWER KEY

Build Your Vocabulary *pages 103–104*

B. 1. medical 2. matched 3. reveal 4. statistically
5. extract 6. diagnose 7. trait 8. concentrated on
9. identical 10. access to **C. Interact with
Vocabulary!** 1. at 2. of 3. up with 4. between
5. by 6. at, for 7. about 8. for, of 9. to 10. and, of

Focus Your Attention *page 105*

A. words and phrases to signal a process: first, and
then, Next, After that

Listen for Main Ideas *pages 106–107*

B. 1. b 2. c 3. b and c 4. b 5. a 6. b

Listen for Details *page 107*

B. 1. T 2. F (will share some of the same genetic
information) 3. F (died in prison) 4. T 5. T 6. F
(not 100 percent) 7. F (6,000) 8. F (might cause a
disease) 9. T 10. T

Talk about the Topic *page 108*

A. 1. River 2. Manny 3. Hannah 4. Manny
B. 1. Expressing an opinion 2. Keeping the
discussion on topic 3. Disagreeing 4. Keeping the
discussion on topic 5. Expressing an opinion

Review Your Notes *page 109*

Answers will vary, but should include the following:
Creating a DNA fingerprint: (box 2) Next, they
extract **DNA**; (box 3) Then they use a **computer** to
read **the DNA** (and use the data to create the profile)
**Comparing DNA from a crime suspect with DNA
from evidence:** (box 1) Scientists take DNA
samples from **a crime suspect**; (box 2) They also
take DNA samples from **the evidence**; (box 3) After
that they design **probes** to see if **the 2 sets of DNA
match**; (box 4) Finally, the more matches they have,
**the more confident police are that they have the
right suspect.**

Take the Unit Test

1. b 2. d 3. b 4. b 5. a 6. c 7. c 8. a 9. b 10. d

UNIT 11 TEST BIOLOGY: DNA Testing

Listen to each question. Circle the letter of the correct answer.

1. a. the many problems with DNA testing

    b. how to create a DNA fingerprint and its uses

    c. how genetic disorders can cause diseases

    d. how doctors use DNA testing to diagnose diseases

2. a. DNA privacy issues

    b. use of DNA testing in crime labs

    c. medical uses of DNA testing

    d. DNA testing on animals

3. a. They share the same genetic information.

    b. They share some, but not all, genetic information.

    c. They are twins.

    d. DNA testing is important.

4. a. They read the DNA with a computer.

    b. They extract the DNA from the samples.

    c. They create a DNA fingerprint.

    d. They see if the samples match.

5. a. to point out that a DNA fingerprint is a reliable way to identify someone

    b. to explain how DNA fingerprinting is done

    c. to explain how DNA testing is done

    d. to emphasize that DNA testing is becoming more common

6. a. how DNA fingerprinting is done

    b. how a crime lab uses DNA profiles

    c. how DNA testing can be used

    d. how the police use evidence

7. a. to create a fingerprint

    b. to identify the victim

    c. to see if they match

    d. to be foolproof

8. a. so that the police will have a stronger case against the suspect

    b. because more probes are needed

    c. so that the police can identify the suspect of a crime

    d. because DNA identification is effective

9. a. certain diseases

    b. a mutation in a gene

    c. a risk for diseases

    d. a link to diseases

10. a. who should have access to the DNA fingerprint

    b. who should own the DNA fingerprint

    c. who should decide how the DNA fingerprint is used

    d. who should be tested

UNIT OVERVIEW

In this unit, students consider concepts related to emergency planning for natural events such as earthquakes. The lecture focuses on creating an emergency plan and an initiative by UNESCO (the United Nations Educational, Scientific and Cultural Organization) to educate children about the risks where they live. The theme is upbeat: "We can't stop (natural hazards). But there are things we can do to try to minimize . . . their impact." Follow-up projects include learning about examples of positive actions taken after natural disasters.

Connect to the Topic *page 112*   *~10 minutes*

Students work in pairs to discuss questions about natural disasters and emergency planning. Students may need help understanding the differences among the different natural hazards mentioned, including tornados, hurricanes, earthquakes, and tsunamis.

Build Your Vocabulary *pages 113–114*   *~15 minutes*

Students study these words and phrases related to public administration and risk management:

allocate	in place	priorities
briefing the public on	involved in	(disaster-) prone
by the same token	the logic behind	the state of being
channel of	minimize	ready
communication	mitigating	targeted
cooperate	numbers of	ultimately
died out	predict	widespread (damage)
ignore	predict with accuracy	

After the Interact with Vocabulary! activity, you may want to have students pair up and practice using the boldfaced words with their partners. Knowing collocations can help students expand their vocabularies and increase their fluency.

Focus Your Attention *page 115*   *~10 minutes*

Students learn to use flags in the margins of their notes to mark information that is unclear to them or that they want to learn more about. Sample notes demonstrate what this practice looks like.

Listen to the Lecture *pages 116–117*   *~30 minutes*

Prior to listening to the unit lecture on risk management and emergency preparedness, students rank six important considerations for a government (Before You Listen). Then they listen to the lecture and answer multiple-choice questions (Listen for Main Ideas) and true/false questions (Listen for Details).
Lecture video time: 6 min. 58 sec.   Number of episodes: 11

Talk about the Topic *page 118* *~20 minutes*

Four students—Alana, Rob, Molly, and Ayman—discuss the lecture. Part A focuses on matching these students with ideas from the discussion. In Part B, your students work on identifying these discussion strategies:

- Asking for opinions or ideas: "So, what did you guys think of the lecture?"
- Agreeing: "Yeah, not only that, but it also . . . "
- Offering a fact or example: "Education, like the UNESCO program, is one inexpensive way . . . "

> **NOTE**
>
> Notice that the comments here may fall under more than one strategy category. The most important point is that students support their opinions with facts and reasons.

For Part C, students are encouraged to use the discussion strategies they've learned. They may use phrases from the student discussion and/or the Discussion Strategy box, or they may come up with their own. Related to the third topic: If students don't know the specifics of the emergency plans in their own countries, have them use the Internet to compile information. This will provide an opportunity to apply the concepts of the unit to their own lives.
Student discussion video time: 1 min. 37 sec.

Review Your Notes *page 119* *~15 minutes*

Students focus on reconstructing their notes, paying attention to questions they want to ask. Encourage them to help each other with the answers.

> **BONUS ACTIVITY**
>
> Ask students to learn about the emergency plan where they currently live. Have them use the five factors in an emergency plan presented in the lecture as a framework to research the natural risks, the channels of communication, and the available services where they live. This is also a good opportunity for vocabulary development as students learn more about the public administration aspect of emergency planning.

Take the Unit Test *Teacher's Pack page 73* *~15 minutes*

You may want to play the lecture again before giving the test. Students answer standard test questions about the content of the lecture. Specifically, the test covers the following: the difference between a natural hazard and a natural disaster, factors in creating an emergency response plan, goals of the UNESCO program, and overall goals of emergency planning.

Extend the Topic *pages 120–121* *~30 minutes*

- Listening and Discussion: Students listen to and discuss a story about three El Salvadorian youths who were trained in emergency preparedness and saved a boy from a mudslide.
- Reading and Discussion: Students read about and discuss what can be done to reduce stress, including the work done by Acupuncturists Without Borders to reduce stress after natural disasters.
- Research and Presentation: Students research and present on a disaster survivor or a relief organization such as the Red Cross.

Focus Your Attention:
Try It Out! *page 115*

Speaker: We're starting to understand how education, especially the education of children, is a vital part of emergency planning for everyone. For example, in 2004, there was a huge tsunami in the Indian Ocean. It affected thousands of people and caused extensive damage. Just as the tsunami struck, a British schoolgirl—Tilly Smith—was on the beach in Thailand with her family. She looked out over the ocean and saw that a tsunami was coming. She yelled to everyone to leave the beach, and she saved many lives. How did she know it was a tsunami? She had learned about it in geography class at school back in Britain. I'm sure her teacher was very proud of her. In December 2005, she was named Child of the Year by a French magazine for what she did. Now, that's one example of one child . . .

Listen for Main Ideas and Listen for Details *pages 116–117*

Public administration lecturer: E1 The topic of today's class is reducing risks from natural hazards. Notice I said natural *hazards*, not natural *disasters*. Natural hazards are events in nature like hurricanes, earthquakes, and tsunamis. We know they can be dangerous, but not all are. There are many small tsunamis and earthquakes we don't even, even notice, and hurricanes that just die out. **E2** By the same token, we know they can create terrible disasters in which many people die and widespread damage is sustained. Three prime examples of this are the earthquake in Pakistan in 2005, Hurricane Katrina in the U.S. in the same year, and the tsunami in the Indian Ocean in 2004. Now all of you remember those, don't you? **E3** Well, today we'll examine ways to reduce our risks from natural hazards so they don't become natural disasters. We can't stop earthquakes or hurricanes or tsunamis. But there are things we can do to try to minimize, or limit, their impact. So, I'm going to divide this lecture into two parts: First we'll look at some of the factors that go into designing an emergency plan. You may be familiar with some of this based on what's in place in your own communities. Then I want us to turn to the role of education in reducing risks to people in disaster-prone regions. **E4** But first, let's go over the terms we'll be using. The first is *disaster preparedness*. "To prepare" means to get ready, right? Preparedness is the state of being ready. Another term is *mitigation*. "To mitigate" means to make less severe, not as bad. We use the phrase "disaster preparedness and mitigation" to talk about what to do to prepare for natural disaster so that the impact will be less severe, and people will suffer less. We can try to lessen, or mitigate, the damage so that people can quickly return to their normal lives. **E5** Now I'll present some factors involved in generating an emergency response plan. First, government officials need to identify the risks. What are the natural hazards? For example, in Japan, there are earthquakes and typhoons; in the U.S., hurricanes and fires. There are several natural hazards in every country. Second, the government needs to establish a channel of communications with scientists. Scientists must be able to share information regularly with the government as they collect data about risks. **E6** Third, government officials need to work out a process for briefing the public on what scientists tell them. The problem is, experts can't predict natural hazards with 100 percent accuracy. For example, they may know a hurricane is forming but can't say exactly when or where it will go. Despite this, public officials still have to decide what to tell the public and when. They can wait and say nothing, or they can tell people to evacuate. If they wait too long, lots of people might get hurt. But if they tell people to evacuate, and then nothing happens, people may get angry. In the future, they may not cooperate. Communicating with the public is a huge challenge for officials. **E7** Here's an example: In 2005, before Hurricane Katrina hit New Orleans, people were told to evacuate. But 61 percent of them didn't. We know some stayed because they had no transportation, no choice. But, of the 61 percent who didn't leave, 37 percent said they simply ignored the order to evacuate. Why? Because they didn't want to leave their homes. Scientific information doesn't do much good if it's ignored. Yet, ultimately, officials must try to keep people safe. **E8** A fourth factor is evaluating what services are needed. For example, are there sufficient numbers of police, firefighters, and emergency workers who are trained to respond to a natural disaster? Is there a network in place for emergency workers to distribute supplies, such as bottled water, food, blankets, and medicine? Is there a way to inform the public about the emergency plan so that they know where to go and what to do before, during, and after a natural disaster? **E9** Well, related to this evaluation is the fifth and final factor: setting spending priorities. Countries have to decide whether to spend money for things they need now, like new schools and roads, or to allocate money to prepare for a natural disaster that may never happen. **E10** Now, let's turn to the role of education in emergency planning. Experts agree that educating the public, especially children, about the risks is essential. Here's one way. The United Nations group UNESCO has launched an international campaign

called Disaster Risk Reduction Begins at School. In turn, many schools in countries like Turkey, France, Mexico, and Cuba now have disaster preparedness and safety programs. The logic behind this UNESCO program is education will help children understand the risks where they live. They'll know specific things to do before, during, and after a natural disaster to make everyone in their communities safer. The hope is that as more children are educated, there will be fewer victims of natural disasters. For example, in Turkey, earthquakes threaten the safety of about 5 million children. So there is now an earthquake education program targeted at students countrywide. And in Cuba recently, with more school programs about hurricanes, there have been fewer hurricane victims. Now that's great news. E11 So, let's review what we've covered today. I mentioned five factors in an emergency plan, and how education of children is considered vital to disaster preparedness and mitigation. I feel a lot of hope now because so many countries see how important a good emergency plan is. Well, that's all for today. We'll see you next time.

Coaching Tips

[1] Critical Thinking: Using your imagination
Have you heard about any of the natural disasters the speaker mentions here? What do you know about them? Think for a minute about what the lecturer has said so far about the difference between "natural hazards" and "natural disasters." Imagine a disaster like one of the examples. How could people manage such a situation to prevent it from becoming a "disaster"?

Find audioscript for the other Coaching Tips at www.pearsonlongman.com/contemporarytopics.

Talk about the Topic *page 118*

Rob: . . . quite a bit.

Ayman: Yeah, so what did you guys think of the lecture?

Rob: Well, I love studying nature, so I thought it was cool. And the idea of hurricanes and everything as "natural hazards" instead of "natural disasters"— that, I think it really helps to understand that nature is dangerous, but not necessarily destructive.

Molly: Yeah, not only that, but it also really makes it clear that people have a responsibility to stay safe, you know? Like, like with Hurricane Katrina in the U.S. back in 2005? Everyone knew the dangers involved, but not everything that could've been done was done, right?

Alana: Well, in a lot of cases, the people aren't to blame for the "disaster" part.

Ayman: Yeah, yeah, like look at earthquakes—how can someone be responsible for something so unexpected?

Rob: Well, but, actually, scientists do know the regions where earthquakes are most likely. So you could say that in those communities people should be building stronger houses and buildings.

Molly: Yeah, what was the, the word that the lecturer used for that kind of preparedness?

Ayman: Oh, I've got, I've got it: mitigation— "making less severe, not as bad."

Alana: In a perfect world, yes, but do you remember the last factor he mentioned?

Rob: Oh, in the emergency response plan?

Alana: Yeah.

Rob: Spending priorities.

Alana: So, money's probably a big reason why some hazards become "disasters."

Molly: Well, that might be true, but I think education, like the UNESCO program, is one inexpensive way to make a really big difference.

Rob: Yeah.

Ayman: Yeah—like teaching people about the risks and to prepare for their own safety. I agree—I think it's priceless!

Rob: Yeah.

Molly: Yeah.

Rob: I mean, so long as the information gets to them.

Molly: Uh-huh.

Rob: You know, people need to be told . . .

Take the Unit Test

1. Which of these topics does the speaker *not* discuss?
2. What is the speaker's main point?
3. Why does the speaker emphasize the difference between a natural hazard and a natural disaster?
4. What is the main goal of disaster preparedness? Choose *two* answers.
5. What is another way to say "identify the risks in a country"?
6. Why does the speaker think the government and scientists need a channel of communication?
7. Why does the speaker mention that experts can't predict natural hazards with 100 percent accuracy?
8. What will happen if the public doesn't know the government's emergency plan? Choose *two* answers.
9. Why is it difficult for governments to set spending priorities?
10. What is the biggest benefit of the UNESCO education program?

Extend the Topic *page 120*

Reporter: Good afternoon, we've been talking about preparing children for natural hazards. Today we have with us Ramon with the Community Emergency Committee in El Salvador. He has some great stories. Thanks for joining us today, Ramon.

Ramon: Thanks for having me. Yeah, I've got a few stories. One that stands out in particular is these three teenage boys who saved a seven-year-old boy named Oscar.

Reporter: Wow. What happened?

Ramon: Well, this is back when El Salvador was hit by Tropical Storm Stan, if you remember that. And at that same time, the Santa Ana volcano erupted. So, as you can imagine, this was a huge emergency situation. Something like 70,000 people had to be evacuated from that area because of the mudslides and flooding. There was mud and water everywhere.

Reporter: Gee. Sounds terrible.

Ramon: It was. But fortunately, a lot of the kids in that area had been educated on what to do in an emergency. Oscar, the seven-year-old I mentioned? So, he was caught in the mud—totally stuck, could not move. It's up to his shoulders when these three teenage boys come along, see him there, totally caught. So they start scooping up the mud with their own hands and fingers, fast as they can. They lift him up, scoop him out of the mud, just in time. These three boys risked their own lives doing this!

Reporter: Wow. Heroes. They must've been scared, though.

Ramon: Sure, but they knew what they needed to do. They'd been educated on how to act in an emergency . . .

ANSWER KEY

Build Your Vocabulary *pages 113–114*

A. 1. c 2. a 3. b 4. d 5. b 6. c 7. a 8. d 9. c 10. a 11. b **B. Interact with Vocabulary!** 1. By 2. out 3. in 4. with 5. of 6. of 7. in 8. behind

Focus Your Attention *page 115*

A. *Answers will vary.*

Listen for Main Ideas *pages 116–117*

B. 1. b 2. c 3. c 4. b 5. b 6. b

Listen for Details *page 117*

B. 1. T 2. T 3. T 4. F (hurricanes and fires) 5. T 6. F (37 percent of the 61 percent who stayed—or about 23 percent of the people of New Orleans) 7. T 8. F (because natural disasters don't always happen) 9. F (to make everyone safer) 10. F (Turkey, France, Mexico, and Cuba)

Talk about the Topic *page 118*

A. 1. Rob, Molly 2. Rob, Molly 3. Alana 4. Rob, Molly, Ayman **B.** 1. Asking for opinions or ideas 2. Agreeing 3. Offering a fact or example 4. Asking for opinions or ideas, Offering a fact or example 5. Offering a fact or example

Review Your Notes *page 119*

I. event in nature, e.g., earthquake, hurricane, that can be dangerous v. serious problem for people, caused by a natural hazard

II. Factor 1: government officials identify risks in their country (or area); Factor 2: gov't sets up communication with scientists so they can share information; Factor 3: gov't sets up procedure for how to share with the public what scientists tell them (difficult because can't predict 100% when event will occur / + people ignore information, e.g., Katrina); Factor 4: evaluating what services are needed before, during, after an event; Factor 5: setting spending priorities **III.** A. educate children to help everyone; B. earthquakes in Turkey, hurricanes in Cuba

Take the Unit Test

1. d 2. c 3. c 4. a and b 5. c 6. b 7. b 8. a and d 9. d 10. a

 **TEST** PUBLIC ADMINISTRATION:
Risk Management

 Listen to each question. Circle the letter of the correct answer.

1. a. the factors in an emergency response plan

b. why disaster preparedness is important

c. the role of education in emergency planning

d. the causes of natural hazards like tsunamis

2. a. There are natural disasters all over the world.

b. Every country should identify its natural hazards.

c. We can't control nature, but we can limit its impact.

d. Scientists should communicate with the public.

3. a. to point out where natural disasters occur

b. to point out that natural disasters are hard to predict

c. to point out that natural hazards don't always cause disasters

d. to point out that there are many types of natural hazards in the world

4. a. to help people return to normal life quickly

b. to know the risks in a region

c. to understand nature better

d. to reduce government spending

5. a. identify the government officials

b. identify the supplies needed

c. identify the hazards that are likely to occur

d. none of the above

6. a. It would help them set priorities.

b. It would help them share information.

c. It would help them reduce risks.

d. It would help them evaluate services.

7. a. to explain that there are many natural hazards

b. to explain why communicating with the public is a challenge

c. to explain why hazards vary from country to country

d. to explain which government services are needed

8. a. The public won't know what to do during a natural disaster.

b. The government will tell people to evacuate.

c. The government will communicate with scientists.

d. People might get hurt.

9. a. because they need many things, like roads and schools

b. because there are too many natural hazards

c. because they can't predict if or when a natural disaster will occur

d. both a and c

10. a. that children learn how to respond to natural hazards

b. that children go to school

c. that children learn about natural disasters

d. that children learn in countrywide programs